Taraṇyali Tridhā Dhyānam: The Threefold Meditations of the Thunder Dragon

Sundernāth (Shandor Remete)

This edition first published in 2022 by
Shadow Yoga
www.shadowyoga.com

National Library of Australia
Cataloguing-in-Publication data:
Shandor Remete
Taraṇyali Tridhā Dhyānam:
The Threefold Meditations of the Thunder Dragon

ISBN 978-0-6455109-0-4

Set in 8.7 on 11 Acumin Pro
Printed and distributed in Istanbul, Turkey
by Golden Tortoise

Disclaimer
The creators and distributors of this book shall have no liability or responsibility to any person or entity with respect to any loss, damage or injury caused or alleged to be caused directly or indirectly by the information contained in it. The information presented in this book is in no way intended as a substitute for a teacher. Before beginning any of the exercises described in the book, you should first seek the advice of a medical practitioner.

Acknowledgements

Editor: John Evans
Graphic Design: Detour Design, Adelaide
Illustrations: Alexandra Hoàng Gilbert
Chapter Illustrations: Simon Buttonshaw
Photography: Bryan Dalli

Dedication

I dedicate this book to the memory of the gurus who, through their great effort and compassion over millennia, have woven the fabric of this yoga. I dedicate it to my *dikṣa* guru Yogin Mahant Narināth who passed the thread on to me at the time of my initiation at the Goraknāthi temple of the Mrigasthali of Kathmandu. Without his blessing this work would never have come into existence. I bow to him in reverence.

Yogin Sundernāth

Contents

	Preface	8
	Introduction	10
Chapter 1	**The Prāṇam and the Five Gurus**	23
Chapter 2	**Taraṇyali Krantam:** The Emerging of the Thunder Dragon	43
Chapter 3	**Taraṇyali Kriyā:** The Proceeding of the Thunder Dragon	65
Chapter 4	**Taraṇyali Dīpa Dhyānam:** The Floating Lamp Meditation of the Thunder Dragon	91
	Conclusion	113
	Bibliography	116

Preface

This work is the accumulation of information gained under the guidance of those rare masters who remain like a handful of small islands in the vast growing ocean of watered down practices that constitute the *haṭha yoga* of this present era. Everything described here has been put into practice and lived through directly, while bearing the burdens of karma and the process of its dissolution.

The ultimate goal of this book is *bhavatita dhyāna* (transcendental meditation). This ancient yoga, the yoga of absorption or *laya* was taught by Adināth and when mastered can be practised at any and all times, whether standing, walking, sitting, eating or sleeping. Meditating on the void (*śūnya*) with no object of focus for support, absorbed in the solitude of space or *lakṣya-titha-lakṣya* (the aim beyond aim) is *bhavatita dhyāna*. This is the heart and soul of *Amanaska Yoga* (yoga without mind) and the best of all *sādhanas*.

The journey to that goal described here, the *Taraṇyali Tridhā Dhyānam* – the Threefold Meditations of the Thunder Dragon, is a complete system of meditation, the roots of which lie in the practices of the Pāśupata Tantrika yogins. The Pāśupatas were one of the earliest tantrika groups and arose in the ancient Harappan civilisation of Mohenjo-daro. They worshipped Lord Śiva in the form of Paśupati, the Lord of the Animals, and were famed for their practice of 'wild dancing' (the *Śiva Tāṇdava*). This dance was used to induce a state of trance, which was then redirected to seated meditation employing the practices of *prāṇāyāma* and *mudra*. The Nāth-Siddhas, accomplished adepts who emerged in medieval times, were the true successors of the Pāśupata Tantrika Yogins, and established the practices of *haṭha yoga*. This knowledge was transmitted to us by the great lords of Nāth tantric haṭha yoga, Adināth, Matsyendranāth and Gorakhnāth, and others, whose stories are told in the first chapter of this book.

This journey of no return is only for those *sādhakas* (practitioners) who possess the necessary strength and courage to complete it. It is of the utmost importance that they choose the most auspicious time to begin. Their task may be compared to the climbing of a sheer ice-covered cliff with no aids but the skill of one's limbs and an unwavering mind. The aim is the awakening of the *kuṇḍalinī śakti*, the coiled sleeping power, through *khecarī vidyā*, the science of the roaming gatherer on the paths of heaven. Great exertions must be made to acquire *uṇmani śakti*, the trans-mental energy that purifies and empowers the central pathway for the rise of *kuṇḍalinī śakti*. This is imparted by the deity directly or through the guru, and the secret of this transmission is conveyed through the 14th *adhāra* of the moon termed *saumya* (placid beyond aims).

At the beginning of a journey, stripped bare in the awareness that you have no idea of what is to come, you stand at a most powerful place. This feeling must never be lost, for as soon as you extend one foot to make a step you move into a divided state of being.

Yet if you stay centred in this truthful void, the steady open mind required for the journey will be maintained. This will allow you to adapt spontaneously on the path without compromise.

Success requires a firm resolution that the mind will not be permitted to deviate from the path; for the *sādhaka* will constantly be challenged by doubts and the evils that accompany them. To overcome these doubts, guidance is required from one who has already gathered this knowledge. Such a guide must be happy and without disease, a master doer, not merely one who is learned. He or she must be an adept or siddha who perceives this world as moving and unmoving, not distinct from his or her own soul.

Introduction

The three processes or phases of the *Taraṇyali Tridhā Dhyānam sādhana* are as follows:

Taraṇyali Krantam: The Emerging of the Thunder Dragon
Taraṇyali Kriyā: The Proceeding of the Thunder Dragon
Taraṇyali Dīpa Dhyānam: The Floating Lamp Meditation of the Thunder Dragon

The first two stages are active; the greater part of the *Taraṇyali Krantam* is carried out standing and the greater part of the *Taraṇyali Kriyā* is carried out seated. The third and final stage of mastery is *Taraṇyali Dīpa Dhyānam*. This stage is passive and is the giver of *mahāsukhādhara* – the subtle form of great ease. The *Taraṇyali Tridhā Dhyānam* is a complete system of meditation from first step to final mastery. The *tri* in *tridhā* (threefold) refers not only to the three stages of the discipline, but also contains a hidden reference to the three energies held in the coils of *śakti* that support (*dha*) this process. These three energies are those of Saraswatī – the goddess of sound, Lakṣmi – the goddess of kindness and the three achievements, and Durgā – the power principle. The additional half coil symbolises the force that drives the energies of creation, sustenance and destruction through to renewal.

The instruments used to access these powers are clearly delineated by Guru Matsyendranāth in his *Matsyendra Samhita*. The five remarkable instruments innately designed for this purpose and manifesting in a natural manner are as follows:

1. *Kuṇḍalinī* – the spontaneously arising coiled power
2. *Suṣumna* or *avadhūti* – the central channel
3. *Jiva* or *go* – the tongue, cow (sacred life). *Jihva* is tongue/ *jiva* is life
4. *Talvādhāra* – the upper palatal support
5. *Brahmarandhra* – the courtyard of the creative principle.

He explains that the first of these enters the second while the third enters the fourth. This fourth then splits and enters into the fifth.

After embarking on this *sādhana* the yogin should only do this yoga, avoiding all other sciences like *japa* (chanting meditation) or *homa* (fire ritual), and should stay free from dualities by raising the tongue and taking it into the plane of *Trikuteṣa Śiva*. Guru Matsyendranāth was supremely generous and compassionate in bestowing the gift of this five-step process. The first instrument is the power, the second is its pathway, the third its instrument, the fourth its entry gate, and the fifth is its arrival. What is disclosed here is the *khecarī mudra* and its central and crucial role. In his conclusion to the *Matsyendra Samhita*, the great master stresses that this yoga is a distinct path with clear and defined practices. This is a warning for those times when the yogin is faced with difficulties on the path and it is easy to be distracted by gimmicks (many of which he lists) in hopes of a quick fix. It will instead lead to disaster.

1. Taraṇyali Krantam:
The Emerging of the Thunder Dragon

The opening of the *Pāśupata Sutras* describes a sequence of methods of worship that provides an overview of this first phase.

Hasita gīta nṛtta ḍuṅḍuṅkāra namaskāra
japyo 'pahāreṇo' patiṣṭet

One should worship with laughter, songs, dance, sounds of dun dun, salutations, mutterings and offerings. Laughter and songs refer to the mental and emotional setting up of the practice. The term for this crucial preliminary is *prāṇam* or obeisance and is described in the first chapter.

The dance that follows is *nṛtta* or pure dance – performed solely to bring about a state of trance and integration.

Namaskāra japyo 'pahāreṇo' patiṣṭet indicates the one-pointedness of mind required to achieve sense withdrawal from the objective world so as to approach the deity with humility, offering oneself with physical, verbal and mental acts fully into the fire of worship. This standing practice prepares for and leads to the seated and prone practices of *āsana-krama* and the physical acquisition of the *khecarī mudra* that completes the process of the *Taraṇyali Krantam.*

2. Taraṇyali Kriyā:

The Proceeding of the Thunder Dragon

Of the three stages of the *Taraṇyali Tridhā Dhyānam*, this is the most difficult to work through. By comparison, the Emerging Step of the Thunder Dragon is smooth and straightforward, since a state of trance is accessed right from the beginning. Mastery of that stage provides the *sādhaka* with the state of mind and the strength and health of body required for the second stage. One who reaches this point must also equip themselves with the appropriate tools for this next venture and understand how to put them to skilful use.

To succeed in this, one must be well versed in, and possess practical knowledge of, the following subjects:

The 10 *prāṇas*
The 16 *nadīs*
The sound systems of the *yoginī-nyāsa-vidhim*
The seven *cakras*.

In addition, one must know the sequence of procedures (*kuñcika krama*) for the step-by-step development and unfolding of the *khecarī mudra*, the soarer of the pathways of heaven. It is this which unlocks the door to the beyond through the dynamic force of the goddess Kuṇḍalinī, in her three fold aspect as *tridhā* - Saraswatī, Lakṣmi and Durgā. This leads to the crowning heights of the *śāmbhavī mudra*, the benevolent gesture of *śakti*.

Although the sequence of yogic activities is conventionally arranged as *āsana, bandha, kriyā, mudra, prāṇāyāmakṛtvā, pratyāhāra, dhāranā* and *dhyānam*, when one enters the stage of Taraṇyali Kriyā the understanding of *āsana* must change.

Up to this point *āsanas* have been done to strengthen the body parts and render the physical form firm and healthy enough to endure what is to come. From this point onwards only a few seated *āsanas* are used and, in essence, these are mild versions of seated mudras.

Siddhāsana, the seat of adepts, and *baddha padmāsana*, the bound or tied lotus seat, are to be used in the processes to activate the pranic force. By implication, this means that all the physical preparations of *khecarī mudra* have been completed.

The three *bandhas*, (ties or locks) can be acquired either through muscular contractions imposed by the mind, or as the natural outcome of the cultivation of *gorakṣāsana, kandāsana* and *bhagāsana (mūla bandhāsana).* This takes longer but as the three *bandhas* spontaneously manifest at the different stages of respiration, the mind is kept in a passive and natural state of reflection. *Nauli kriyā* entails the manipulations of the abdominal recti in circular or pumping modes. This is an important process as it not only purifies the upper and lower abdominal cavity, and improves the energy of the throat by reducing damp heat and phlegm, but also, and more importantly, it influences the *baṅkanala nadī*, the curved conduit within the upper brain.

Nauli kriyā will only produce its full benefits once the seat *vajra-mudrāsana* has been mastered and with it, full control of the *vajra-nadī*. This mastery is crucial to gain the full benefits of all the *bandhas* and *mudras* (the gestures of bodily and mental attitude) that engender and then bring control over the inner energies of the life wind, and thus, of the mind.

The importance of the *khecarī mudra* has been stressed by many texts. The *Haṭha Yoga Pradipika* states:

There is only one mudra - khecarī.

The Jayadramalaya Tantra says:

The mudra called khecarī is the queen of all mudra kings

and the Tantra Loka states:

Of all mudras she is most important since
in essence Khecarī is a deity.

It is clear from the first statement that the other *mudras* will not yield their full benefits unless the science of *khecarī* has been mastered. The second statement indicates that the other *mudras* are masculine, in other words, physical in nature, while the *khecarī* is feminine and therefore subtle. The last affirms the statement in the preface of this book that the *uṇmani-śakti* or trans-mental energy required to trigger the rise of *kuṇḍalinī śakti* is imparted by the deity directly or by the deity through the guru. That deity is Khecarī, the queen of all *mudras*.

In conclusion, one can say that when the nose, eyes, ears and the tip of the tongue meet at the *talvādhara*, the 10th support and seat of Lord Yama, then that ancient spirit, by the power of his soft swaying, creates the sound of harmony, *haṃsa*, the swan of Saraswatī. The cessation of this sound marks the moment when Śakti (the power that drives the processes of yoga) dissolves into Śiva, who saved the world from the *kāla-agni*, the dark destructive fire and restored the harmony of the natural state, the *sahaja-avasta*. There is much here for the *sādhaka* to pay attention to and reflect on. What is certain is that the work with the *mudras* requires patience and endurance in the face of discomfort and uncertainties both on the physical and mental planes. The suggested period for processing these challenges is a minimum of 16 years, depending on the unique karma of each individual.

Prāṇāyāmakṛtvā refers to the practice of breath control. *Prāṇa* refers to the wind (breath), that moves in and out through the mouth and the nose. Control refers to suspension of the breath, which is a function of the *puruṣa*, the self. Success in breath control must be preceded by knowledge, desire and effort. One should be seated in *baddha padmāsana* and begin the suspension of the breathing process either after exhalation (*recaka*), or after inhalation (*pūraka*) or through retention, (*kumbhaka*) of the vital breath – *prāṇa*. This must be maintained until one feels that the breath is under control and that one is absorbed in meditation.

By the practice of prolonging the gaps after exhalation and inhalation over a long time, one will slowly overcome the urge to breathe. This is the inner retention of *prāṇa*, the vital breath, in which one has the experience of complete fullness without a feeling of heaviness.

The gaining of this control is apprehended as the currents that operate through the peripheral channels begin to draw towards the core and into two of the three main *nadīs*, the *lalana* and *rasana* (*ida* and *piṅgala*). As the control and that inner flow increase, then the current approaches full absorption in the originating sound, the *haṃsa*, within the central path of the void, the *avadhūti nadī* (*suṣumna*). Then one reaches a state of purification and complete withdrawal of the senses. By maintaining this, the state of *pratyāhāra* is obtained and if it is further prolonged it evolves into *dhāranā*, the state of one-pointedness of the mind. A longer period of practice causes the mind to be reabsorbed into the pranic force. When the *prāṇa* dissolves back into its source, the individual self, then the state of meditation, *dhyāna*, is at hand.

The process of gaining control of the breath must be steady and measured. The unit of measurement used is the *mātra*, the time taken to blink the eyes (literally, a measure or unit). The duration of *kumbhaka* (retention of breath) is divided into three levels of intensity - weak, medium and intense (*adhama*, *madhyama* and *uttama*). *Adhama* is 20 *mātras*, *madhyama* 24 *mātras* and *uttama*, intense, is 30. These specifications vary a little from school to school.

Although the term *prāṇāyāmakṛtva* can be simply translated as acquisition of lengthening of the life force, further division gives other layers of meaning. *Pra* stands for the vital breath, *ana* refers to breathing, *an* to posture and *yama* to tying, implying not only control of vital air though mastery of the whole body, but also the withdrawal of the senses, renunciation and the destruction of sin. *Kṛ* means to do, *tva* means several, suggesting the multiple activities within this process since *prāṇāyāma* performed with *mantra* multiplies the benefits. Reflection on this will make it clear that the different practices and stages of the yogic path are woven together with the thread of the pranic force. All these stages together with their allotted practices, instruments and skills are aimed at bringing the vital energy under control in a natural manner. In the realm of the vital force, attempts to force the process or neglect these stages will lead to the premature end of the journey and the death of the practitioner.

3. Taraṇyali Dīpa Dhyānam:
The Floating Lamp Meditation of the Thunder Dragon

As we have seen, the second stage of the Thunder Dragon is a set of *vikaraṇa* or transformations that brings the changes in physical and mental states required to enter the pathway of light that leads to the end of the journey of self-cultivation.

The Floating Lamp Meditation corresponds to the 16th *adhāra* (support) that is activated on the day of the full moon. The suggestion is that through observing the energy of the full moon, one can receive guidance as to how to proceed towards completion of the journey to light. The pathway rests on the wings of *haṃsa*, the power principle of the breath, and the floating lamp is its peak.

The first step of the *Taraṇyali Dīpa Dhyānam* is to acquire practical knowledge of the process by which the energy of the 24 *nadīs* or accumulation sites is gathered into the central three channels. *Lolana* (solitary *lola* [swayer] of the tongue), *rasana* (giver of the essence of taste) and *avadhūti* (central pathway and giver of the form of great ease) provide the primary foundation of sound, wind and light and are responsible for the development of all the energies and their fields. The 24 power accumulation sites that range between the hairline and the knees are the conduits of the highest bliss, and are divided into three groups of eight, the *nadīs* of illumined mind, the *nadīs* of illumined speech, and the *nadīs* of illumined form or *bindu*.

The cultivation of the practical science of the *nadīs*, fields and primary central channels, is accomplished through the practice of *yoginī-nyāsa-vidhim* (the placement of power through touch).

The skilful and responsive application of this science together with all that has been mastered in the first two phases brings the *sādhaka* to the crowning procedures of the *śāmbhavī mudra*. *Śāmbhavī mudra*, the gesture of the benevolent form of Lord Śiva, is acquired through seven stages that manifest spontaneously. The sequence and manner of these manifestations confirm the *sādhaka's* location on the path, just as the stars and planets rising in the night sky are used for navigation.

The spontaneous aims (*lakṣya*) and gazes (*dṛṣṭi*) determine the direction of the individual's development, and their seven stages are clearly outlined within the text of *Amanaska Yoga*. This text is traditionally attributed to Gorakhnāth, but there is controversy among Sanskrit scholars about this attribution because of what are viewed as contradictions in the texts. Speculation about textual differences is not profitable for the practitioner. For my part, I agree with the commentator Yoganāth Swami, that Gorakhnāth is the author since, unlike these scholars, he is knowledgeable about the texts and is an accomplished practitioner.

The tools of scholars are textual analysis and textual comparison, but these methods alone do not provide sufficient understanding of the processes described to make judgements about the functions of and relationships between the practical activities they explain. Only lived experience of the process of unfolding will reveal the nature of the transitions and how tools that once served the *sādhaka* so well must be discarded, since not only are they useless in the stages of development that lie ahead, but also they will in fact block access to them.

For those who lack experience of the full course of yogic *sādhana*, the method and philosophy set out in the *Matsyendra Samhita* and then expounded in the *Amanaska Yoga* may appear divergent and contradictory. However, to one who understands the stages of unfolding, the *Matsyendra Samhita* gives what is to be done, while the *Amanaska Yoga* explains how to perceive that which arises from this course of action. Guru Matsyendranāth sets out the technical procedures, while Gorakhnāth shows how to receive the outcome and grow with it, hence his famous statement, 'the guru and I are one'.

In the eighth chapter of his *Samhita*, Matsyendranāth explains that internal worship will bring the *śāmbhavī* state and he goes on to describe it:

Then the yogin should accomplish homa within himself; perform sacrifice into the inner fire with offerings of the imagination. The yogin who adores Śambhu, immaculate and of the form of ātman (soul) becomes united with the prosperity of the empire of yoga. Thereafter, there will be no more obstacles to internal worship.

The soul should be worshipped in the mūlādhāra which fills the horizon with the brilliance of the light of a thousand young suns, pure, untainted, matchless and nourished by its own power.

Matsyendra Samhita 8.45 -49

It is the outcome of this process that is described in *Amanaska Yoga*:

Only one whose sight, breath and mind remain fixed and stable without the support of objects is a true yogi. He is a guru and worthy of service.

Amanaska Yoga 2.46

It will be clear from this brief outline of the Thunder Dragon Meditations that great patience is required to endure the difficulties and hardships that will arise. To negotiate these obstacles, the *sādhaka* must possess great faith, courage, adaptability, and the capacity to take risks. Only great effort backed by tremendous willpower will bring success.
The demanding requirements of this path are repeatedly stressed in the texts. One such warning states that those wishing to become *siddhas* (adepts) are as numerous as the black crows that gather in flocks, but those who succeed are as rare as the white raven. Many fall away distracted by fame or glory. Others blame their teacher when difficulties arise that reveal their own shortcomings. Some fall because of impatience, while others cannot break their attachments to the mundane activities of the herd. A few falter when they are only one step from the goal, which results in the same outcome as if they had never started out on the path.

To avoid these pitfalls one must learn the skills of the craft of light through a process of natural adaptation. In this way one can remain on the path without fear that one's energy will run short before the portal to the beyond is reached.

If one reaches that gateway one must still remain cautious, without wishing for anything since one cannot know what is waiting on the other side. This is the meaning of the story of the death of Ravana, the King of Laṅkā. When he was awarded immortality by Lord Śiva for his austerities he asked only for protection from the gods, demons and animals, but not from humans. This is why Lord Viṣṇu took a human form as Prince Rāma to kill Ravana, so as to put an end to all the havoc he had brought to the world of beings.

As Ravana was dying he said to Rāma: 'Did you think it was through stupidity that when I was given immortality I did not include protection from humankind?'

The moral of this story is that one should never hanker after or obsess about perfect scenarios or imagined outcomes, since even wonderful powers like immortality can prove a curse. It is important to leave an opening, just in case one steps into something that one cannot adapt to. True wisdom is to maintain one's direction but free of agendas and investments, and to do only what needs to be done, neither more nor less, to adapt to what arises on the path. This is the power of the *siddhas*, the adepts.

Khecarī clears the pathway for *kuṇḍalinī* but one must learn the wisdom of living with it and understand that the very difficulties and obstacles that arise on the way will provide the experience and knowledge to clear the way to the heights of wisdom. At those heights, that wisdom is of light and without shadow or form. For this reason, although one may start meditating through forms or on images of Śiva, those meditations must end objectless and beyond form (*nirviṣaya* or *nirbīja*). Due to mastery of the path of forms and formlessness through austerities, the *siddhas* have the freedom to choose whether to depart as mortals, or to continue on as an immortal until they decide to leave the earthly plane of existence.

Chapter 1
The Prāṇam and the Five Gurus

Prāṇam or obeisance is the essential beginning of every action on this path. It is a necessity because of the intractable illusion that arises over and over again in all humans. The great sage Krishna Dvaipāyana Vyāsa expresses it best in a statement that should be set in front of all initiates before they embark on the perilous journey of self cultivation:

The greatest wonder in the world is that we are all mortals and yet live like immortals.

Prāṇam is a bow of respect in prayer, but to whom and for what purpose? The dual meaning is hidden in the two terms used to discriminate actions - *parasmaipada* (for another) and *ātmanepada* (for self). The *prāṇam* is addressed to Lord Śiva and those great ones who preceded us, but also to the in-dweller, the Self whose seat is the *ajña cakra* and who is known as Śrihatta, the residential ruler of the *kula* (the inner 'community'). *Prāṇam* is the sequence of obeisances given to the gurus in order to receive their guidance and their gifts. The nature of these gifts is hidden in the iconography and narratives of the gurus which are codified within the prayers. By bringing all this to mind the *sādhaka* is directed towards the goal of their quest, for all that is referred to lies latent within their own being. In this way, the *prāṇam* corrects distortions in attitude and establishes the required mindset for the journey and it must be done prior to the practices of any yogic *sādhana*. The verbal mutterings of *prāṇam* are also the first step on the long journey towards the inner sound. This journey is best described in the *Janeu Mantra*:

I bow my head to the Guru, whose virtuous nature rests in the wisdom of truth, the giver of instruction, to him I bow with respect.

Oṃ Guruji, on entering the void, in the beginning, raising the sound AUM, that removes suffering and gives accomplishments, the accomplished one brings the thought of sound to a point.

The sound of the moon, the sound of the sun, sound stays completely within the body, in the heart, in the soul, in the mind.

The soul is small, the immense is smaller than the smallest amount.

The shape of sound is an illusive puppet show spectacle. The manner to shape it is to make one point, BINDU. Sound, point and yogis have the same behaviour (Nad-Bind-Yogin).

It is apparent that struck sound happens, that sound is playing, time is running, beyond is the benevolent ascetic guru, the protector of the tongue - Gorakṣa who is decorated with the hat of wisdom, that grants one to tie the frivolous loose hair of the demonesses, Ḍākinī and Śaṅkiṇī who are the causes of decline.

Receiving this wisdom removes the suffering from the quadrangular dwelling place of Lord Śiva, freeing the four powers of life at the mūla cakra, the abode of power.

While the Yogi plays the sound and recites the mantra he is fed 36 kinds of elixirs.

The Yogi can play the sound without the mantra, but the three worlds of the body will remain devoid of sound.

The one who knows how to pierce the one pointed sound, does it alone and becomes one with God.

Twilight is Śiva's eternal time of dwelling, where the siddhas who are the masters of their stringed instruments, assembled through the successive ages.

Therefore the wisdom of mantra is complete.

Knowing this much of sound I bow to Śri Nāthji Guruji, I bow.

For the beginner entering the *Taraṇyali Krantam* the sequence of prayers within the *prāṇam* is as follows:

1. The inner invocation of the 24 main *nadīs* or accumulation points that form three fields of inner power that fuel the flame of illumined wisdom. These are the eight pathways of the enlightened mind, the eight pathways of enlightened speech and the eight pathways of enlightened form.

2. The invocation of Śri Gaṇeśā, the remover of obstacles and the blesser of beginnings.

Oṃ Śri Gaṇeśāya namaḥ.

3. The invocation of Adināth (Lord Śiva) – the first teacher, in union with his power Śakti, the source of the stream of wisdom.

Oṃ ādināthaṃ namāskṛtyam
śaktiyuktam jagadguruṃ namaḥ

I pay obeisance to the first guru,
Lord Śiva united with Śakti,
the preceptor of the universe. I bow!

4. The invocation of Matsyendranāth – the Lord of the Fishes, who holds the power to restore and purify the minds and bodies of practitioners.

Oṃ śri guruṃ matsyendranātham
varabitihastaṃ kiritadhyaṃastam
yadiyam svarupaṃ vikarairvyudastam
mano' yesya bhūtanukampadisatām
sadā yogi matsyendranātham nataṣṭam

I bow to Matsyendranāth
Whose right hand gives the gesture of fearlessness,
Whose left hand holds the trident of beneficence.
Through his perfect form,
The auspicious restorer and purifier of deformities
In the minds and bodies of his devotees.
I salute you O vast eternal yogi, Lord of the Eight Directions.

5. The invocation of Gorakṣanāth – the protector of practitioners and unfolder of the secrets of the waxing and waning cycles of the moon that enable the cultivation of the pranic force.

Oṃ gorakṣabhālaṃ guruśiṣyapālam,
śeṣāhimālaṃ śaśikhaṇḍabhālam
kālasya kālaṃ jitajanmajālam,
vande jaṭālaṃ jagadābjanālam

All praise to Gorakṣa who gives protection
And the lustre born of yoga to gurus and disciples,
the crescent moon on his forehead,
the great serpent Śeṣa as his necklace.
Killer of time and conqueror of birth and death.
Bearer of this whole world as the stalk is to the lotus flower.

Adināth

Adināth is Pāśupatināth transfigured as the first Lord Guru and protector of the Nāth-Siddha yogins. They worshipped him as Adināth, Anamaḥ (the nameless), Alakh (the unseen) and Anādi (the unborn).

In some texts the first five human gurus are described as having been born from different parts of Adināth's body:

1. Matsyendranāth was born from his navel.
2. Gorakh (or Gorakṣanāth) from his head.
3. Jālandharnāth from his bones.
4. Kanipanāth from his ears.
5. Cauraṅgīnāth from his hands and feet.

In this way, knowledge intended for initiates alone is transmitted through *saṇdhyā-bhāṣa* (twilight language).

Matsyendranāth

Matsyendranāth's title, 'Lord of Fishes' comes from the legend in which he is swallowed by a giant fish. Matsyendranāth spends the next 12 years perfecting his yogic *sādhana* (practices) in the belly of the fish. With mastery of these practices he is able to free himself, and is depicted in the dance position (*karaṇa*) called *bhujaṅga lalitam* (swaying serpent) as he tears his way out of the fish's abdomen. In another depiction, Matsyendranāth is shown in a more advanced version of this *karaṇa* called *khecaram* (wanderer of the paths of heaven).

Upright with inner heels touching, toes turned outwards and palms placed crossed on the lower abdomen, the human form resembles a fish standing upright on its tail. This image represents the composed human being in the process of detaching their consciousness from the restrictions of mundane life.

Since the navel is the seat of the sun within the human body and the centre of digestion, freeing himself from the belly of the fish through prolonged yogic practice signifies that Matsyendranāth has gained mastery over thirst, hunger and sleep. He thus rules over the *rasana nadī*, the subtle channel of the essence of life, the pathway of the sun and one of the three most important subtle energy pathways within the body.

So Matsyendranāth was born from the navel of Adināth, but also received guidance through the innate light of consciousness that lies in all of us. The question is, can one awaken from the slumber of indulgence in food-related attachments through the concentrated power of will?

When the significance of his name and origin is grasped and when he is worshipped within at the *nabhi cakra* (the seat of the sun), this prayer transmits the complete nature of Matsyendranāth and his gift to mankind.

Gorakṣanāth

Gorakṣanāth is the first disciple of Matsyendranāth. Although the word Gorakṣa commonly refers to a cowherd and Gorakṣanāth is popularly known as the Lord of the Cows, *'Go'* can mean cow and tongue and it is the latter translation that indicates his true nature. Initiates refer to him as Śri Aum, Protector of the Tongue and Herder of Thoughts, indicating that he is a master of *khecarī vidyā*, the hidden science of *kuṇḍalinī yoga*.

His body is of the colour of the full moon and his dwelling in the human body is at the junction of the three *nadīs* where the tongue is turned back to enter the cavity in the roof of the palate called *vyomacakra* (centre of void). He represents purity of mind and patience. He rules over the *lalana nadī* (solitary channel), and is the sole lord and master of the secrets of the crescent moon and its cycle of waxing and waning.

He is depicted in the *karaṇa* called *ūrdhva-jānu* (raised knee), and his seat is *mukta padmāsana* (loosened lotus), one of the seats recommended for the prolonged practices of meditation.

Jālandharnāth

Jālandharnāth's title is Holder of the Net. A contemporary of Matsyendranāth, he was, like him, initiated by Adināth. Jālandharnāth was a powerful magician and famed for his ability to take on any bodily shape he chose.

His seat is in the base of the throat and when this area is mastered one gains power over all the bones, and through its connection with the ears, control of both the heat and all the fluids in the body. The *jālandhara bandha* of tantric haṭha yoga, which gives primary control of this area, is named after this master.

This bandha is one of the crucial means by which yogins achieve their goal. Jālandharnāth is depicted in two *karaṇas*, *nikuñcitam* (shrinking or shrivelling) and *talasamsphotitam* (burst plane).

Kanipanāth

Kanipanāth was a disciple of Jālandharnāth. His name conveys a number of meanings. *Kan* means to shine and *pa*, to protect. The shining referred to is that which arises when the energies of the intellect are gathered together and transformed into *buddhi* – the intuitive consciousness. There is also a hidden reference to *karṇa* (the ear) in *kan*. To convey all this, his name can be translated as 'Protector of the Ear and Intellect'.

The most conspicuous external feature of the Nāth ascetics are their large earrings. These are inserted at the time of their final initiation into the Nāth lineage by splitting the cartilage in the centre of the ears. The exact location in the ear is called the 'zero point', and it is connected energetically both to the innermost cavity of the ears, where the unstruck sound is heard, and to the navel centre. Due to the increased sensitivity this procedure brings, the consciousness is also able to access karmic memory in the inner space of the hollow bones of the body. This location is also responsible for regulating body temperature even in extreme weather conditions.

Kanipanāth studied the science of yoga under his guru Jālandharnāth for 12 years. One day close to the completion of his studies while he was meditating, he heard the sound of angelic voices deep inside his ears. His guru warned him to ignore these sounds, but he was repeatedly drawn into them and each time lost control of his physical body so that he ended up floating like a limbless ghost in space. He kept getting trapped in this cycle until he was finally able to submit completely to his guru's guidance and regain bodily awareness and control of his limbs.

The hidden meaning here is that it is not enough to hear something. Mental recognition is partial. Knowledge must be lived and experienced through the body.

Voices heard within the inner ears, of whatever kind, are mere by-products of the fluctuating intellect. They are never manifestations of the light of consciousness. Yogins who separate wisdom from its means, will surely fall and end up like fools constantly looking for new toys. To avoid this, one must have full trust in one's guide and complete faith in, and full application of, the specific practices and guidance that they give. Only then will wisdom arise.

Kanipanāth is the guardian deity of the *anāhata-nada* (the unstruck sound) that emanates from the spiritual heart of the *anāhata cakra*. True sound is heard within the right ear, and the echo of that resounding in the left ear is the manifestation of the *kuṇḍalinī śakti* in its fullness. The end point of all intellectual endeavours is reached through the rising resonance of the cosmic sound AUM.

Without sensitivity to this phenomenon, and however carefully the fingertips are placed to adjust the flow of air in the name of *prāṇāyāma*, all one achieves is torture of the nose.

Kanipanāth is depicted in the *karaṇa* called *kuñcitam* (crawling into).

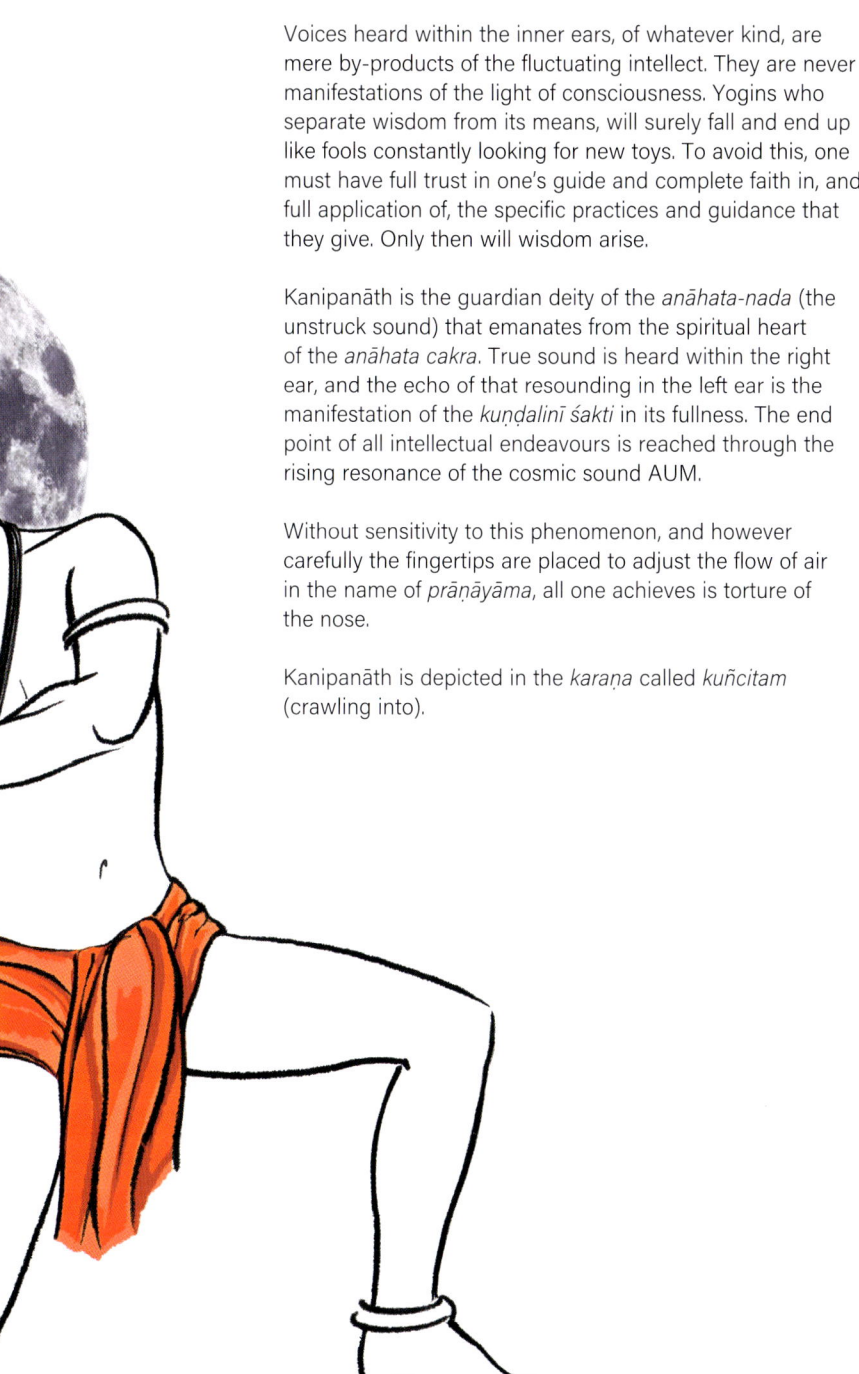

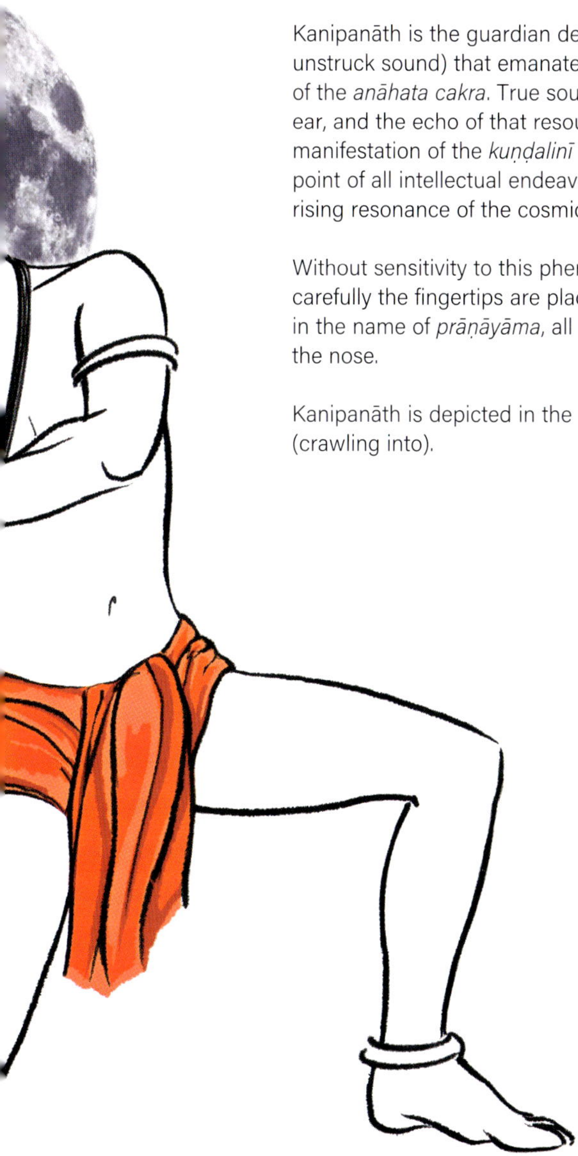

Caurangīnāth

Caurangīnāth, whose name means 'the man whose limbs were stolen', was the son of the Chola King. Unfortunately, his mother passed away when he was 12 years old and, after his father remarried, his stepmother wove a web of deceitful stories to discredit him. Eventually these angered his father so much that he ordered the boy's hands and feet be cut off at the wrists and ankles and that he be taken out and left in the jungle to be devoured by wild animals.

Fortunately Caurangīnāth was blessed with good karma and Matsyendranāth happened to pass by the tree under which the Chola prince had been laid out to await his dreadful end. The great master took pity on him, became his *dikṣa* guru and initiated him into the central channel breathing technique. Matsyendranāth assured him that 12 years of this practice would restore his limbs.

With these words, the Lord of Fishes vanished from the scene, not to return until the the completion of those 12 years. Gorakhnāth took on the role of his *upadeṣa guru*, whose function is to attend to the needs of the student and oversee their practices. After completing the 12 years of *tapasya* (austerities), Caurangīnāth rose up, began to dance and then flew away. He is always depicted in the *karaṇa ānanda tāṇdava* – the wild dance of bliss.

The knowledge hidden in this narrative is profound. The first 12 years of life constitute an age of innocence when the child is nurtured in the lap of mother nature; in yogic terminology, the *kuṇḍalinī śakti*. At the end of this period, as the hormonal secretions of adolescence begin to flow and transform the body, the intellectual powers begin to unfold. With the rise of the intellect (the stepmother), the intuitive trust for mother nature is dispersed and the confidence of the child shaken. Into this vacuum steps the controlling father, the ego or *ahaṃkāra* (literally, the I-maker).

So the child (the soul) is forced to protect itself. Some run, some hide, while others find a disciplined activity and a teacher so that they can gather and direct the scattered energies within.

The severed hands and feet represent the state of the average person beginning yoga, in whom natural spontaneity of body and mind has been disrupted by the self-consciousness of adolescence.

The conscious reintegration of the movement of the limbs is the first step in regaining what has been lost and this is accomplished through mastery of the *tāṇdava* (wild dance).

This gives rise to a trance state as the limbs and core come alive as a single unit. The Chola prince became an immortal through his austerities but never passed his knowledge on to another person, instead giving it to the tree that gave him shelter so that that tree became immortal.

The narratives and iconography of the five gurus awaken the dormant spiritual intuition and also reveal crucial information about the process of teaching and learning on this path. It sets out the five important regions of cultivation in the human form and indicates how they can be utilised to gain control over the powers within to remove obstructions and overcome ill health. The lore of Matsyendranāth and Gorakṣanāth indicates how control can be gained over the physiological, psycho-emotional and intellectual faculties. The Jālandharnāth iconography reveals the network of subtle energy pathways within the neck and throat and how the physical structure of the bones can be harnessed.

The Kanipanāth story uncovers the role of the cavity within the ears where sensitivity to the unstruck sound is developed and where control can be gained over the eight channels operating through the physical heart. The Cauraṅgīnāth story indicates that it is only through the cultivation of hands and feet, wrists and ankles that the neck and waist are freed and the spinal column rendered agile and adaptable for all conditions. This creates an unobstructed energetic course for the life force to traverse up and down this heavenly highway. Only when all five of these areas and their associated functions are regulated is one equipped with a fit vehicle for the long and difficult path, littered with pitfalls, that lies ahead.

Armed with this knowledge, one is able to select the most fitting instruments, whether *karaṇa*, *āsana*, *prāṇāyāma*, or *mudra*, to achieve the appropriate step in the cultivation of each of these five regions.

This method of discrimination frees one from the burdens of ignorance and greed that otherwise condemn the aspirant to lose themselves in innumerable methods and techniques with no idea of goal or process. This is the warning that lies behind the description of the 8,400,000 postures of yoga from which only 84 are recommended for human use, out of which 32 are the best, of these, 16 most favourable, and only two are supreme.

As this understanding is sadly lacking in the present world of so called yoga, the efforts of nearly all are obsessive, chaotic or mechanical, driven by sensation and brute force. Such efforts can only lead to failure and regret or fantasies of liberation built only on that shakiest of foundations – emotion.

Caurañgīnāth represents a beginner *sādhaka* in possession of a pure heart who, in a single-minded state of attention and with senses withdrawn from the objective world, offers himself or herself with all physical, verbal, and mental functions as a servant stands with gifts before their master. In this manner and with the shining intuitive intellect as their protector, they begin the secret passage of trance that is hidden within the actions of *nṛtta sādhana* – pure dance, the first stage of the *Taraṇyali Krantam*.

Chapter 2
Taraṇyali Krantam: The Emerging of the Thunder Dragon

The *nṛtta* described in the *Pāśupata Sutras* is part of a method of worship, an internalised *puja* or ritual process. Initiated through prayers to Adināth and the Nāth gurus, the *nṛtta* is performed as an *upacāra* (an offering through invocation to the deity). However, for the *sādhaka* to utilise it in the spirit of Cauraṅgīnāth as the first step of the Taraṇyali Krantam, he or she must understand the method and goal of this practice. If this is fully grasped and manifested it will lead them smoothly into the practice of *āsana*, *mudra*, and *prāṇāyāma*.

In his commentary on the *Pāśupata Sutras*, Bhagavan Kaundinya describes the movements of the *nṛtta* dance as:

. . . rising and sinking, expansion and contraction of the hands, feet etc. not in a way conflicting with the convention of dramaturgy.

He makes clear that while the outer appearance should conform to the dance of the theatrical arts, the inner purpose is very different. The *Abhinaya Darpana* of Nandikeśvara, considered the most ancient text on dramaturgy, describes *nṛtta* as pure dance, devoid of emotional content, in contrast to *nṛtya*, which conveys emotion, and *natya*, which combines all the elements to present narrative. The same text also distinguishes between three modes of dance. The *nṛtta* of the *tāṇdava* used in yogic *sādhana* utilises the *laghu* or 'light' mode. This form is considered 'light' because it is completely devoid of the emotional projection and theatrical intent that characterise the *vikata* mode and the acrobatic performance of the *viṣama* mode.

The sole focus of the *nṛtta sādhana* is to rediscover the life currents hidden within the body by means of unimposed natural rhythmic movements.

Indian dance is created by assembling component shapes and short movements called *karaṇas*. The *karaṇa* (literally, action/doing) is the instrumental form of transformation and 108 of these are described in the traditional scriptures.

Only some of these are appropriate for yogic cultivation and only a few are required for the *nṛtta sādhana*. A grouping together of these chosen *karaṇas* is termed an *aṅgahāra*.

The *karaṇa aṅgahāras* are characterised by fluid stepping and spiralling footwork, with subtle swaying movements of the torso that flow into *hasta mudras* – gestures of arms, hands and fingers. The rhythmic coordination required to achieve these forms demands intense concentration on the movements of hands and feet. It is easy for the mind to become trapped in the manipulation of this surface activity and it is crucial for the yogic *sādhana* that the inner goal is kept in mind and the manner of engagement directed towards that goal.

This offering must be made with every cell of the body, and the key to achieving this is given in the fourth chapter of the *Matsyendra Samhita* in the description of the *yaśasvinī nadī*.

The yaśasvinī nadī has many branches and spreads from the tips of fingers to the tips of toes.

Matsyendra Samhita IV. 50

The objective of the *nṛtta sādhana* is the full expression of this *yaśasvinī* current that permeates the body so that it reaches to the extremities of the hands and feet. When the body is integrated through this current in rhythmic swaying movements that resonate with the pulsation of the core, a state of pure action ensues, the surface mind becomes void and the inner light dawns. The origin of this pulsation is the electromagnetic pumping of the cerebrospinal fluid that synchronises the pumping of the ventricles of the heart and governs respiration. When these rhythms are harmonised through the *nṛtta sādhana*, then external respiration ceases and inner respiration begins. In this way the inner movement of the pranic force is completely freed from external disturbance or states of *vata*.

The implication of the Cauraṅgīnāth story is that as long as the person is consciously manipulating the limbs, however exquisite their movements or gymnastic their feats, the hands and feet remain cut off from the consciousness. It is the lack of this understanding that leads to so much wasted effort in the circles of contemporary yoga. The same lack of understanding lies behind the current fixation with and misuse of *ujjayi* breathing.

The term *ujjayi* means victory but victory over respiration is not gained by squeezing the throat or forced loud breathing; this gross imposition leaves a person as separate from their breathing as they are from their limbs.

In the early stages of practice, achievements of the state of resonance and the inner light it brings are short lived as the connection is very easily lost. The periods of connection are experienced as short gaps in the fluctuating activity of the mind. It is during these gaps that the proper movement of the life force manifests. As skill and sensitivity develop, these gaps begin to lengthen and the life force is deepened and extended. This extension of the life force is the true meaning of *prāṇāyāma* and this is where the *sādhaka* is learning to make the connections necessary for the practice of *prāṇāyāma* in the next stage of Taraṇyali Kriyā. Once the connection to the inner current and inner resonance is stabilised, a single unbroken flow streams all the way to the tips of the fingers and toes, and one gains not only a state of equilibrium and health, but also an unbroken and complete experience of the light of one's being. As the 12-year period in the story of Cauraṅgīnāth's rediscovery of his limbs suggests, this will not be achieved in a short time.

Clearly, this is not a practice for the rough beginner but only for those who have been sufficiently prepared and tested. If the gross patterns of behaviour have not been worked through, then the information in the texts and stories will not come alive and cannot be applied in action. If the main obstructions in the physical structure have not been removed, then the *karaṇas* cannot be accessed.

Oṃkāra – the entry gate

After the *prāṇam* and the *panca caraṇas* (the movements of the five 'wanderings' that activate the joints), the initiate performs the *Oṃkāra* (the *japa* of the syllable *Oṃ*). *Oṃ* is the integrated form of all sounds, all cosmic vibrations and the sacred bearer of the supreme light of consciousness transmitted to us through the sun and moon in the form of fire. Therefore, the uttering of *Oṃ* should be undertaken before beginning any auspicious undertaking. The practice is apparently simple and straightforward, requiring a 27 bead *mālā* (rosary) and the ability to squat at ease and with steadiness. The squatting position used is *pūrṇa maṇḍala* (full circle). *Ardha maṇḍala* (half circle) is a less intense position and is also acceptable to begin with. However, if neither position can be held for the necessary time and in the required manner, it shows that the preliminary work has not been completed and embarking on this journey is premature.

Once established in the posture, the *mālā* is held in the right hand while the left hand is used to count the rounds of the *mālā*. The *japa* (muttering) is performed in silence while the mind reflects on the qualities of sun, moon and fire and their corresponding qualities of action, will and wisdom. The *japa* is performed with the whole body and the inner experience is absorbed by the whole mind. By the end of the *japa* of 16 rounds of 27, the seed sound of light has been uttered inwardly 432 times. When 4, 3 and 2 are added together the universal number nine is obtained. This represents three multiples of three – sun, moon and fire; action, will and wisdom; and body, mind and soul. This practice establishes all the *prāṇas* but crucially the *apāna vayu* and so prepares the body for the *nṛtta karaṇa aṅgahāra*. However, if basic conditioning of the limbs has not been accomplished this gate to the *nṛtta* cannot be entered.

If *japa* can be performed in the squat it indicates that one is able to raise and lower the body with ease so that the central breathing mechanism is not disturbed. This requires freedom not only in the ankles, knees and hips, but also in the groin and armpits so that the side and floating ribs remain relaxed throughout all movements. Without this, the internal respiration cannot begin; instead, breathlessness leads the surface mind to engage and impose artificial forms to support the emotional states that arise. For most modern-day aspirants much preliminary training will be required to reach this point.

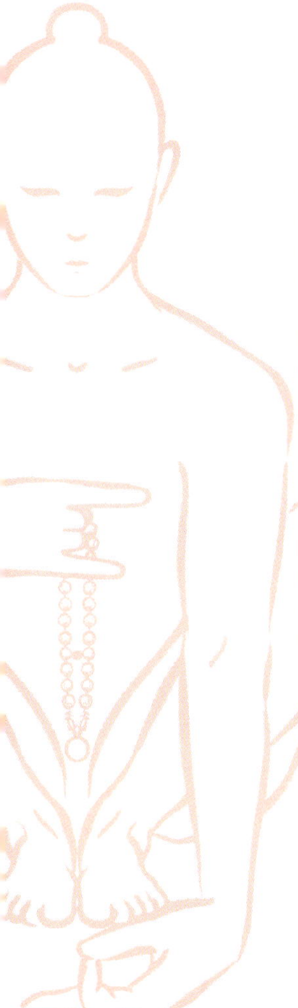

Varāhi kanda aṅgahāra

The *karaṇa aṅgahāra* used for the Taraṇyali Krantam is the *varāhi kanda*. *Varāhi* is the female boar deity; she is *śakti* in the form of the sow, Protectress of Earth, and the Earth Mother. *Kanda*, the bulbous root, is the source of all the *nadīs* and is linked to the sixth petal of the second *cakra*, *svādhiṣṭhāna*, which has the resonating vibration LAṂ of the earth. Mastery of the *varāhi kanda* opens this sixth petal called *kanda*, which is the gate to the *kanda-sthāna*, from which rises the three primary *nadīs* - *lalana*, *rasana* and *avadhūti* - the pathway of *śakti* from the *mūlādhāra cakra*. Correct performance of this *aṅgahāra* gives the key to open the entrance for the *prāṇa* into the central path; the pathway of fire, and so provides both form and fuel for the rise of the transcending energy of *kuṇḍalinī*.

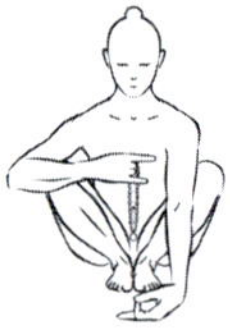

At the completion of the *japa* of *Oṃ*, one remains in *pūrṇa maṇḍala* and performs *bhastrika* (bellows breath) *prāṇāyāma* for three to six minutes, or to one's natural limit, and then rises to the half squatting stance called *utkatāsana* and performs *nauli kriyā* (described later) for up to six rounds.

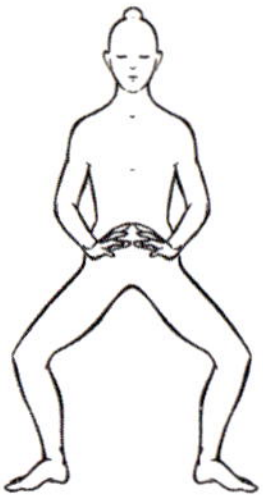

Then one assumes *vaiśaka*, the causal form which also means the form within the formless. One must stay in this *karaṇa*, building up to a duration of one gati - 24 minutes, until one gains an unbroken flow of energy from the tips of the fingers to the tips of the toes, with the inner breath smooth, long and thin, accompanied by an unbroken, soft and barely audible sibilant sound.

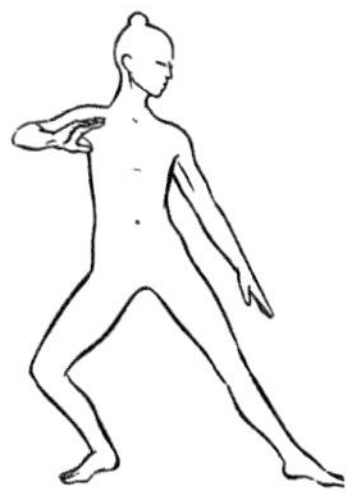

From here, one enters *varāhisthāna* (the wild boar stance) and performs 16 rounds of its movement

and continues into *ardha svastikam* (half sun wheel)

to *ūrdhva tāṇdava* (wild rising)

to *yalikrantam* (the dragon's step)

to *cakramaṇḍalam* (closed circle/circuit)

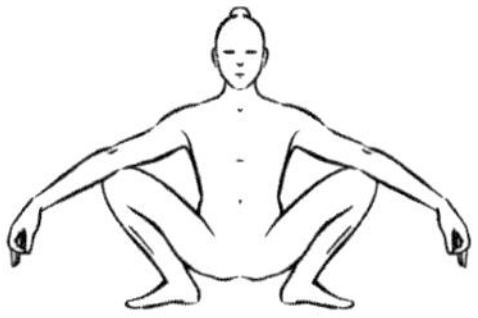

and finally into *ardha maṇḍalam* (half circle in *vaiśaka*).

The internal process of this sequence of *karaṇas* is as follows. The central power is made to move to the extremities of the limbs in *varāhi*; it is intensified and circulated via the Half Sun Wheel, Wild Rising and Dragon's Step. The power is locked in with the Closed Circuit and then sunk into the base, the *kandasthana*, through the Half Circle squat. This last inner shift brings the mental poise of trance, that must be sustained and directed towards *pratyāhāra* - sense withdrawal, and *dhāranā* - concentrated mind. This progressive taming of the mind continues with the seated practices of *āsanas* that are instrumental in nullifying all mental constructs, and establishing the first layer of *dhyānam* - meditation.

Āsana-krama

Āsana-krama is the method of unfolding of the *āsanas* (postures). The *āsanas*, like the *karaṇas*, are manifestations of *āṅgika abhinaya*, the creation of natural forms through the combination of arrangements of the body parts. These parts are *śiras* - head, *hasta* - hands, *vakṣas* - chest, *parśva* - the sides of the chest, *kati* - the sides of the waist and *pada* - the feet. The secret powers of both *karaṇas* and *āsanas* are hidden within the skilful placement of these parts to achieve different shapes with the body, which by their inner nature alters the movement of the life wind through the different *nadīs* (channels), purifying and rendering them free from obstruction, and eventually leading to the *avadhūti*, the fiery pathway of *kuṇḍalinī śakti*.

There are no special techniques or gimmicks, whether physical and external or energetic and internal, to gain entry into these different shapes.

The unique energetic nature of each *āsana* is the spontaneous outcome of the form itself. The mindset of entry determines whether the outcome is bad due to forcing beyond one's limit, or beneficial, accompanied by a blissful feeling of robust health, lightness and wellbeing.

Therefore the *karaṇas* and *āsanas* are the practical folding and unfolding of the body's six 'limbs' in action in a step by step manner, for the increase of power leading to the spontaneous awakening of the core power of life, the *kuṇḍalinī śakti*. With this attitude the understanding grows that one is dealing with the releasing, increasing, gathering and binding of the outflowing energy of the pranic force; the internalising of that force and eventually condensing it first into a single pillar and then to a point called *bindu*. That *bindu* is the alchemically prepared elixir – the fuel that takes one beyond the clutches of form and time.

The key to this alchemical process is the combined action of the famed *khecarī* and *vajrolī mudras* that gives rise to the state of *śakti calanī mudra*, the gesture of deceiving the mind. This is a sphere of great intensity and power and if the preparatory activities have not been done following correct guidance and in a thorough manner, one will be faced with dire consequences, which can end in insanity or even death.

The *Taraṇyali Krantam*, the Emerging Step of the Thunder Dragon, is the preparatory ground for that alchemical process. The goal is to strengthen and integrate the limbs of the body into a centralised structure that will be able to endure the difficulties of tempering and centrally binding the pranic force.

The *āsanas* required for this cultivation are as follows and in this order. They are entered from the *ardha maṇḍala* squat, at the end of the *karaṇas*.

Makarāsana
Ūrdhva mukha and *adhomukha śvānāsanas*
Vajrolī mudrāsana
Gorakṣāsana
Udarkandāsana
Maricīdaṇḍāsana
Bharadvajāsana
Jade Lady Waving in *mukta padmāsana*
Baddha padmāsana
Yoga mudrāsana
Tolāsana
Nauli kriyā in *mukta padmāsana* with *bhastrika*
Garbha mudrāsana
Kukkuttāsana
Śavāsana

On Saturdays and days of difficulty, the practice should be restricted to *bharadvajāsana*, *maricīdaṇḍāsana*, *gomukhāsana* and *vajrolī mudrāsana*. This will be sufficient.

Makarāsana

Makara is the mythical sea creature, the water dragon, the *vahana* of the goddess Ganga, and the sea god Varuna. The *vahana* of a deity is usually described as the mount or vehicle but it represents a divine attribute, a hidden quality or gift that if accepted, carries the being effortlessly upon the waves of their destiny. In this case *makarāsana* stabilises the water element within the body, making it as smooth as the surface of a lake with the powerful currents under the surface freely operating to sustain the legs' balance without disturbing the body's equilibrium. *Makarāsana* is the precursor of *bhujaṅgāsana* and its variations. *Makarāsana* is performed lying on the stomach and has two variations, one with straight legs and the other in *padmāsana*. It is a mild back arch and works on the lower regions of the abdominal wall. *Ūrdhva mukha śvānāsana* and *adho mukha śvānāsana* together create a kind of pumping action that is used to exit and enter other *āsanas*.

Udarkandāsana, Gorakṣāsana and Vajrolī Mudrāsana

These three *āsanas* enhance the natural responses to the three *bandhas* of *uddiyana*, *mūla* and *jālandhara* during the phases of respiration – the exhalation and its following pause and transition, and the inhalation and its following pause and transition. When the *bandhas* begin naturally to respond at the appropriate junctions in the cycle then exhalation ends spontaneously in *uddiyana bandha*, while inhalation begins with *mūlabandha* and ends in *jālandharabandha*. This is the natural rhythm and when one is in tune with this, one can develop these natural skills and manipulate the processes of the life wind to gain voluntary control without imposition.

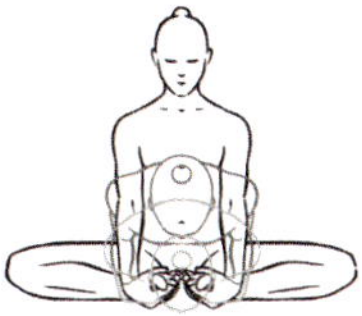

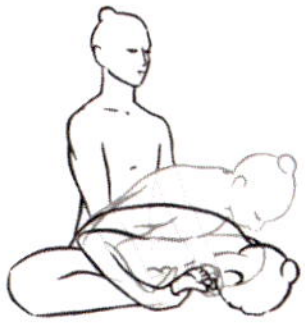

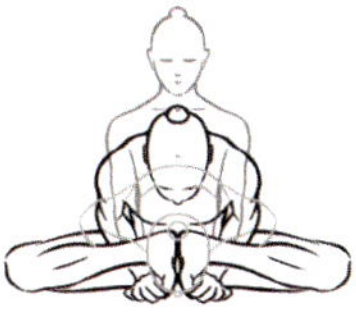

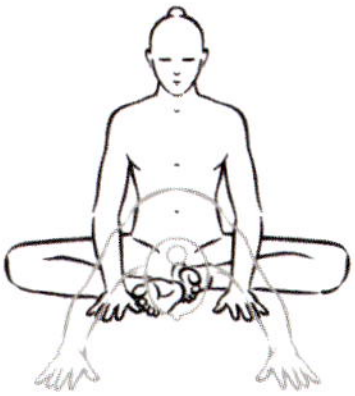

Maricīdaṇḍāsana

This posture frees the body of disturbed wind – *vata*, clearing the mind of its burdens due to the unobstructed flow of the pranic breath.

Bharadvajāsana

The form of one of vigorous bearing. Bharadvaja was a *ṛṣi* (sage) of Aghora, the non-terrifying face of Lord Śiva. Although on the surface it is only a mild seated twist, it is extremely difficult to access its benefits. It fans the fire (*agni*) and burns up the remaining unwanted *vata*.

Jade Lady Waving

This is a *kriyā* (process) of hand and arm work performed in *mukta padmāsana* (loose lotus) for the enhancement of the pranic force. Maintaining and directing the energised state when moving from the standing activities to the seated practices is a great skill and many fall into dull or mechanical behaviour. The practice used to navigate this transition is called the Jade Lady Waving.

Jade Lady is another name for the *kuṇḍalinī śakti* and in this practice a long sequence of rhythmic movements is carried out in a seated position. The seat used is *mukta padmāsana*, or the loose lotus, and the weaving consists of swaying, waving and spiralling motions carried out through hand gestures with movements of the arms, head, neck, waist and trunk coordinated from the hips, but with the lower extremities held still.

Although the movements of the Jade Lady are similar to those in the *nṛtta sādhana*, the rhythm is much slower. While the *nṛtta sādhana* is performed at a natural 'strolling' speed, the movements of the Jade Lady are slowed down to a minimum. Through this slowing down every part of the body can be drawn into action. The activity is then conducted through the bones and joints, keeping the soft tissues toned and smooth instead of relying on muscular tension and pumping actions.

In this way, the subtle forces latent in the physical body engage and the *sarvāṅga* state is achieved. *Sarvāṅga* (literally, all limbs) does not merely indicate the sum of the component parts of the body, but that since the body is a microcosm of the cosmos, when every cell in the body is engaged, the divine within it is made manifest. When this is revealed in one's own body one is ready for the finer stages of cultivation.

At this stage, the *sādhaka* experiences the arousal of tremendous heat within the body while the head remains cool. This signals the triggering of the posterior channel – the *avadhūti nadī*, and from this moment the movements of the body direct the inner circuit of the breath so that there is no need for external respiration. If the need for external breathing arises it is an indication that a fault has surfaced in the practice. The completion of the full form takes about half an hour.

Baddha-padmāsana – the bound lotus posture

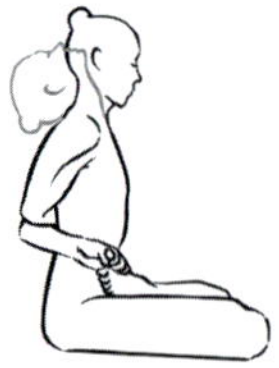

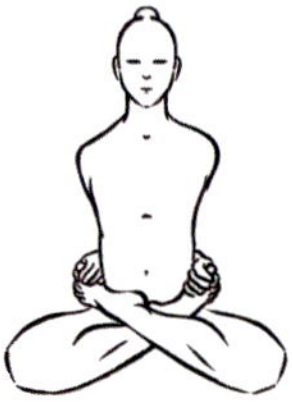

In his text *Gorakṣa Śatakam*, Gorakhnāth uses the term *kamalāsanam* for this *āsana*. Kamala refers to the lotus flower used in the worship of Śiva and is also one of the names of Lakṣmi. This is an indirect reference to *kuṇḍalinī śakti*. Gorakhnāth recommends this *āsana* for the practices of *prāṇāyāma*, which indicates that mastery over *khecarī*, *vajrolī* and *śakti calanī mudras* is part of this *āsana*. Mastery of this *āsana* means that one is no longer in need of respiration of the external air, but is able to conduct the pranic breath through the three main channels of moon, sun and fire, increasing the light and heat and eventually centralising it. In this way, the pathway of *śakti* is freed within the binds of this *āsana*.

All 16 *nadīs* are tied in to the central circuit and the three *bandhas* naturally respond at the appropriate time and in the appropriate places during the circulation of the *prāṇa*, while the tongue controls the opening and closing of the gates of the channels of moon, sun and fire.

The importance of this *āsana* cannot be overemphasised since once it is mastered, the rest of the journey can be followed with ease.

Yogamudrāsana

This is the key to bringing the circulations of the life force to a standstill, which is the beginning of the rise of *bindu*. Once this *mudra* is mastered, the need for *mahāmudra*, *mahābandha*, and *mahāveda* will disappear.

Tolāsana

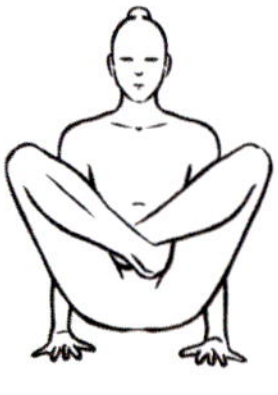

This removes the heaviness that can result from *yogamudrāsana* in the early stages of its practice.

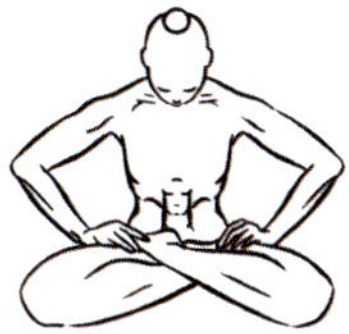

Nauli Kriyā

This refers to the isolation of the rectus abdominus, a churning action in three phases from left to right then from right to left and finally a central pumping action. It is performed in *muktapadmāsana*, preceded by *bhastrika prāṇāyāma* for three to six minutes, and is performed during *recaka kumbhaka* – exhalation retention. *Nauli kriyā* is crucially important for the success of *śakti calanī mudra*, through the shaking loose of the door to the rise of the Goddess of Nature, Kuṇḍalinī, from her slumber. This activity must be learned gradually over a period of at least six months from a guru who is an expert in this field. The combined churning and pumping actions should total 1000 per day (500 during the sunrise session and the same again at sunset). The secret of success is in the slow, systematic building of endurance. This cannot be learned from books or through copying an image or video. Besides its health benefits, it purifies and strengthens the 16 important channels and the field of consciousness, including that of the mind. Unless *nauli* is mastered the following *āsanas* and *mudras* will not yield the required results.

Garbhamudra

The gesture of the embryo aids in centralising the actions of the life breath so that all three *bandhas* are activated simultaneously.

Kukkuttāsana

The cock posture removes heaviness and sluggishness from both body and mind, rendering them calm and at ease yet alert like the cock when it crows.

Śavāsana

The posture of the corpse performed with the alertness of the wisdom of consciousness is crucial for the removal of *rajasic* and emotional fluctuations. When this is mastered, respiration ceases and the solitude that results gives rise to the mindset required for *mantra sādhana* (which follows).

Khecarī Vidyā
Preparatory practices

Preparation for the *khecarī mudra* is two-fold: daily recitation of the *khecarī mantra* is carried out in parallel with the the physical preparation for the *mudra* (described below), so that the *sādhaka* will be properly equipped for the full utilisation of *khecarī mudra* in the next stage, the Taraṇyali Kriyā. This is the entry into the complex and refined science that is termed *khecarī vidyā*.

The *āsana krama* described above is followed by 108 *japa* of *khecarī mantra* in *mukta padmāsana*. This must be performed while reflecting on the mantra's meaning and be followed by a period of stillness, staying with the resulting resonance until the mind decides it is enough. The basic principles of mantra *sādhana* have already been set out within the *Oṃkāra* practice performed before the *nṛtta sādhana*. Without this practice, the *khecarī mudra* will be devoid of form and power. The crucial role played by *mantras* within these yogic practices is given in the *Matsyendra Samhita*.

In the beginning mantra siddhi (power of mantra), should be achieved by all means or yoga will do no good for the yogin, therefore a wise man should work on chanting the mantras, even if they are not in perfect form.

(Matsyendra Samhita 8: 77-79)

The *bījam* or seed syllables that make up the *khecarī mantra* are as follows:

HAṂ is the seed of *khecarī* in the *ajña cakra*, the third eye.
KAṂ is the seed of the mind in the *anāhata cakra*, the heart centre.
MAHĀCANDA is seed of the great rhythm that flows down with this mantra.
VAṂ is the seed of the *svādhiṣṭhāna cakra*.
RAṂ is the fire seed (*agni bīja*); the power of conscious will in the *nabhi cakra*.
OṂ HUṂ PHAT is the *vajra mantra*, the bearer of the power of thunderous lightning in the *mūlādhāra cakra*.

Therefore, the *khecarī mantra* with *bīja* is as follows:

OṂ HAṂ KAṂ MAHĀCANDA
VAṂ RAṂ OṂ HUṂ PHAT.

This is followed by the *ātma mantra* in which the energy of the main body parts is invoked through touching the key points of power while intoning their associated seed *mantras* for the attainment of all knowledge.

VAṂ PAṂ LÖṂ AṂ RĪṂ AIṂ

The essence of its hidden meaning must be meditated upon both during the silent internal chanting and afterwards while remaining seated in *mukta padmāsana*. The deity of Khecarī is the carrier and wielder of the thunderbolt, whose seed sound HAṂ is the wrathful great terror, which destroys all mental dispositions within the inner grove of the heart. It ignites and purifies the sun-fire that resides there and restores the equanimous state of śiva-nature, so that the soul is released from the delusory slumber of darkness and enters the light of liberated wisdom. When meditated upon, this *mantra* will reveal its true form in a visual experience, and this visual manifestation of light will guide the *sādhaka* safely upon his or her chosen path. Without guidance it is very easy to go wrong on this path and it must be emphasised that *mantra* practice has nothing to do with visualisations or imposed imaginings. The power of *mantra* performed correctly within the process described in the three meditations of the Thunder Dragon will bring this manifestation.

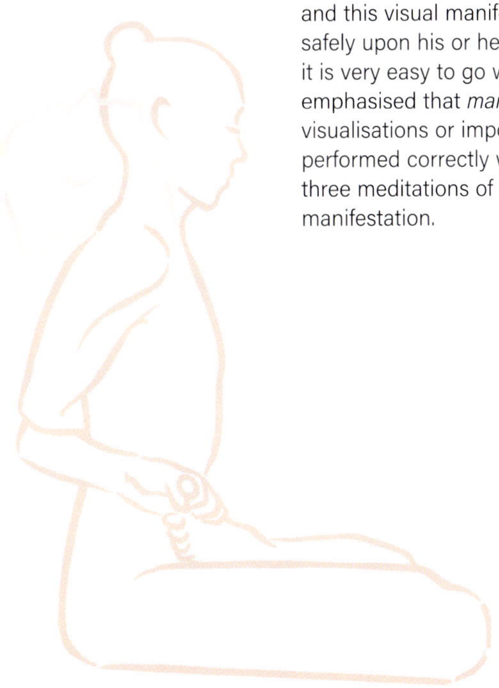

Khecarī Mudra - The physical preparation

The physical acquirement of *khecarī mudra* requires that one thrust the tongue back in the mouth all the way to the end of the upper palate, so that the tip makes contact with the ridge formed by the bone of the base of the skull, and the septum at the root of the nose. To get the tongue this far back and up and to maintain this contact for long periods of time (hours on end) requires thorough preparation, which can take anywhere between three to five years. For most aspirants three years are enough to accomplish this feat, but in some cases there can be stubborn resistance. To achieve it, the tongue has to be lengthened and the frenum lingua must be cut. The lengthening is a hard labour as it must be done twice a day before the practices at sunrise and sunset, and each time requires at least 20 minutes.

The process of lengthening is done using a soft, thin, fine, face towel. One takes hold of the tip of the tongue and pulls it downwards out of the mouth beyond the tip of the chin, then up to the middle of the forehead, from there to the right ear and finally to the left ear. This is one set and one should do 16 sets of this milking each session, and then at its conclusion rub the bottom of the mouth at the root of the tongue clockwise in a circular fashion.

The next step is to place the first digit of the right thumb behind the uvula, hooking it over both the soft and hard palates, and gently pull towards the front teeth making the upper palate flexible. Force must be avoided at all times, otherwise, one will provoke difficulties on the physical, physiological and mental levels that can lead to short-term or irreversible damage. The milking of the tongue and the softening of the hard palate should be done twice a day for six months. Only then can one begin the cutting of the frenum of the tongue. The cutting should be done once a week on Mondays and will take a period of between 6 and 12 months to complete. The best blade to use for cutting is in the shape of a crescent moon (I used a blade like this that I obtained from a plastic surgeon). This will make it easy to be precise in the cutting as each incision should be no thicker than a hair's width. After the cutting, the wound should be rubbed with a mixture of haritaki powder and rock salt.

The wound will heal in a couple of days. The idea behind this repeated systematic intrusion is to send a message to the body that the frenular attachment is no longer needed. If you are observant you will notice that by the end of the first three weeks the frenum has begun to get thinner. Eventually it reduces to half a hair's width and it is at this point that the sinew should be severed. This must be done from behind, not from the front, so as to fully free the tongue from the bottom of the mouth. The frenum is called *kaṇḍarā* in Sanskrit and in addition to this one that attaches the tongue, there is one at the upper lip, one in the heart, one at the male organ at the prepuce, one in the clitoris for the female and one in each arm and leg, making eight in total. It is important to know this, especially when performing the churning of the tongue.

Although I have explained most of the process, I have not described the exact location of the cut, which is crucial. The reason for this is that one should not attempt this process without guidance from someone who has successfully gone through the whole process and who understands all aspects of *khecarī vidyā*. Without that guidance many things can go wrong, especially in the areas of the other *kaṇḍarās* as well as with the eyes, ears, speech and breathing. One must be very vigilant and take great care.

Once the cutting of the frenum has been achieved, the milking of the tongue and the softening of the palate should be continued for two more years with the same intensity. One should also begin to train the tongue to go back using the fingers and the thumb of the right hand. One should slowly enter the upper palatal cavity, all the way to the junction of the root of the nose and ridge mentioned earlier, which is connected with the centre of the third eye. One must learn to block the nostrils with the tongue as this will be used for *prāṇāyāma* in *baddha padmāsana*. Great caution must be exercised here too, since if the process is hurried or forced, damage will occur in the brain, throat, heart, navel, reproductive or excretory organs and defects will arise in the arms and legs. Therefore one must 'make haste slowly' or the rest of the journey will become a nightmare.

One can see that behind all the praise and accolades showered on the *khecarī mudra*, the actual process of conditioning the body for it requires not only tremendous effort from the *sādhaka,* but also great vigilance.

The alchemical texts describe a parallel process in which the term *khecaram* (power of flight) is used to describe the outcome when the essence of mercury is bound and stabilised. A similar emphasis is placed on appropriate timing of the complex processes in the alchemical method. If the compound is heated too fast or before it has been properly prepared and stabilised with the necessary operations, then the essence leaks or evaporates and is lost. The term used to describe this loss is *haṃsaga* (the departing of the swan or goose), and again there is a parallel with the yogic process. Unless correctly bound (*baddha* or *bandha*), through appropriately timed and coordinated yogic discipline, the vital breath or *haṃsa* will eventually escape from the body, resulting in death. Treat this guidance with deep respect and reverence, since it concerns your inner self, and has come to us from the wisdom of great men and women gained though immense effort over millennia.

With this, we end the Emerging Step of the Thunder Dragon, the *Taraṇyali Krantam*.

Chapter 3
Taraṇyali Kriyā: The Proceeding of the Thunder Dragon

According to the *Yoga Kuṇḍalinī Upaniṣad*, the breathing process causes the rise of images within the mind, which suggests that the breath is the physical counterpart of the mind and uses the brain as its tool. Consequently, if voluntary control is gained over the breath, one is able to put an end to the imaginary play of the mind by controlling the field of consciousness, its playground. This is the aim of this second stage of the Thunder Dragon. The *āsanas*, *kriyās* and *mudras* employed here are all procedures used to achieve the above aim in a natural manner, avoiding any imposition from the mind.

This goal is accomplished by choosing those *āsanas*, *kriyās* and *mudras* in which these energetic changes naturally arise so that the mind is attracted and absorbed into them. The consequent transformations of shape and rhythmic patterns of breath that accompany them imprint a complete physical and visual experience on the mind. This keeps the mind centred in the power of the experience, and the power of the experience in the centre of the mind, so that one gains the ability to look into the mind by means of the mind. Once this ability is gained, the *sādhaka* yogin is a master craftsman in the art of self cultivation.

It is no exaggeration to say that 98% of present day would-be practitioners of *haṭha yoga* are little more than frustrated contortionists hanging on to the idea that persistence alone will one day bring them enlightenment.

I am well qualified to say this as I was once one of these diehards with access to, and ability in, at least 90 *āsanas*, including some of the most intense and demanding ones. To this day I have never come across an enlightened contortionist, yet I have seen many who have ended up unable to walk or even lie down. The point I am making here is that the development of wisdom is not gained through a multitude of means, but through a few that have been well chosen. Out of the many one must select those that naturally bring the required results and these are few. The ones that I list here provide the required means and develop the necessary intensity to advance on the journey.

On the other hand, there are others who hide behind the texts that state that all that is needed are two *āsanas* – *vajrāsana* (*siddhāsana*) and *baddha padmāsana* (the bound lotus). These references come from texts which deal specifically with meditation practices and only the *āsanas* associated with them, but their authors knew full well that those seats together with their associated *mudras*, *bandhas* and *kriyās* would have already been mastered though a process similar to that described in the previous chapter. Hiding behind only two *āsanas* is another way of watering down the art and science of yoga and deluding oneself and others.

The *āsanas* required for the *Taraṇyali Kriyā* are as follows:

Vajrolī mudrāsana
Kandāsana
Gorakṣāsana
Bhagāsana (mūlabandhāsana)
Bhujaṅgāsana
Paścimottanāsana
Pūrṇa (or *ardha*) *matsyendrāsana*
Kurmāsana
Pāśinī mudra 1, 2 and *3*
Yoga mudrāsana in *baddha padmāsana* and *mukta padmāsana*
Viparita karaṇī mudra
Sarvāṅgāsana
Halāsana
Karṇapīḍāsana
Matsyāsana
Kapāli mudrāsana.

Kandāsana, Gorakṣāsana, Bhagāsana (Mūlabandhāsana)

Once *jālandhara bandha* (the binding of the throat) has been gained through the mastery of *gorakṣāsana*, the ground has been prepared for *kandāsana*, in which the natural tendencies of *uddiyana bandha* (the binding of the abdominal cavity) naturally manifest. This development then leads into *bhagāsana* (*mūlabandhāsana*) that accomplishes the binding of the womb, the natural shrinking of the inner space of the rectum, and the famed *mūlabandha*, or anal lock. These three *āsanas* establish the basis for all the *mudras*.

Bhujaṅgāsana

After mastering *bhagāsana* and the *mūlabandha*, one should proceed to *bhujaṅgāsana* since *bhujaṅga*, the cobra, is the single-limbed creature that lives in a hole in the earth. It becomes naturally accessible once *mūlabandha* has given control of the elements of earth and water.

Paścimottanāsana

At this point *paścimottanāsana* is done to calm the excitement of rajas that arises with *bhujaṅgāsana* since this *āsana* naturally controls *apāna vayu* and through this, the other nine *vāyus* are drawn into a central point in the *mūlādhāra cakra*.

Pūrṇa and Ardha Matsyendrāsana

Of the spinal twists, only *pūrṇa* or *ardha matsyendrāsana* aid in dissolving the three knots in the *suṣumna* (*avadhūti*) and will make the later practices more accessible.

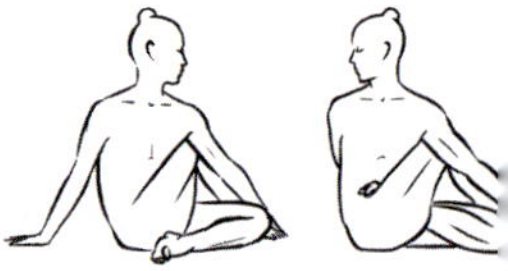

Subsidiary Āsana-mudras

Following *paścimottanāsana*, the *sādhaka* is ready for the subsidiary *āsana-mudras,* which include:

Kurmāsana
Pāśinī mudra 1, 2 and *3*
Yoga mudrāsana in *baddha padmāsana* and *mukta padmāsana.*

Viparita Karaṇī Mudras

By the mastery over this sequence of *āsanas* and bodily *mudras*, the *sādhaka* gains entrance to the *mūlādhāra cakra*. This is the appropriate time to begin that set of *mudras* that helps to open the central pathway for the rise of *kuṇḍalinī śakti*. These are the *viparita-karaṇī mudras* usually described as inverted gestures.

Viparita means reversal, but this can be interpreted in a deeper way to suggest that these are procedures of reabsorption. This insight reveals that these *mudras* are the only tools specifically devised for the purpose of *laya krama*. They are as follows.

Sarvāṅgāsana – all limbs

In addition to a corrective and purifying effect upon the occipital girdle and cerebellum, this aligns all the *cakras*, from the *viśudda* throat *cakra*, all the way to the *mūlādhāra*, and purifies them. It also increases bone density and stimulates the free circulation of lymph.

Halāsana – the plough

Along with the beneficial influence on the excretory and reproductive organs, this intensifies the purifying action of the *viśuddhi cakra* over the entire body-mind complex.

Karṇapīḍāsana – the remover of pain from the ears

This has the same benefits as *halāsana*, but also corrects defects in the ears and kidneys.

Matsyāsana

At the end of these the fish posture is then performed as a preparation for the *viparita karaṇī mudras* that follow.

Kapāli Mudrāsana

This is sometimes called *śirṣāsana* but the meaning of this more revealing and accurate term is 'the communal gesture within the skull'.

All these *mudras* require a highly refined mind, with full responsiveness to the entire 'community' of the body at the minutest level of perception.

This is the meaning behind the use of *sarvāṅga* in the name of the pose commonly called shoulderstand.

The term 'gesture of the community within the skull' contains a hidden suggestion that when this *mudra* is mastered, one will gain control over the cerebral cortex, the cingulate gyrus, thalamus, corpus callosum, septal area, amygdala, pituitary gland, hypothalamus, hippocampus, brain stem and cerebellum. This 'community' also includes the 16 important *nadīs* as well as the curved *baṅkanala nadī* that unites the two channels of the posterior and the anterior sections of the *avadhūti* ((*suṣumna nadī*) that meet at the fontanelle. This is the reason this *mudra* must be positioned and held exactly on the tiny point that lies between the front edge of the fontanelle and the hairline. This is the site of the indivisible *nadī*, the first *nadī* of the group that governs the illumined mind (these are described in detail in the next chapter).

It is from this tiny point that the entire mechanism of the body, together with the empirical mind, are controlled by the master yogin. This is why *kapāli-mudrāsana* is called the king of all *āsanas*, while *sarvāṅgāsana* is described as the queen since it governs all the bodily functions.

Together, the various component parts of *viparita karaṇī mudra* open the gate to *kuṇḍalinī yoga*. This practice is always concluded with *yoga mudrāsana* in *baddha padmāsana*. This prepares the mind and body for the process of *śakti calanī* (described later in this chapter), also referred to as *saraswatī-calana mudra*.

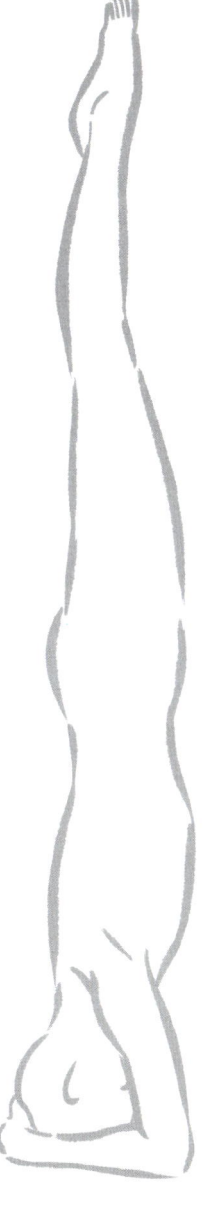

The 16 Nadīs

This is a good place to introduce the locations and roles of the 16 main *nadīs* that form the secret network underlying the *suṣumna*, or *avadhūti nadī*, the central channel of the void of fire.

All but two of these *nadīs* fall into three main groups according to their origin.

A. Seven stem from the *mūlādhāra cakra*:

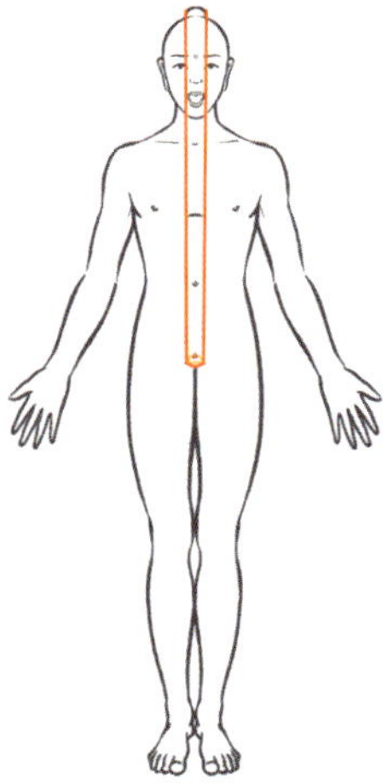

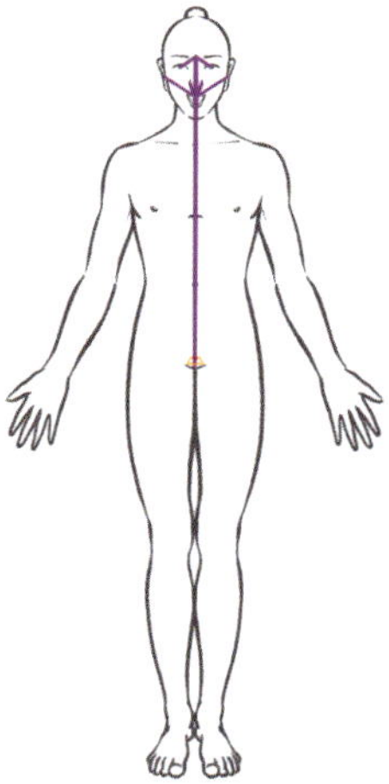

1. *Suṣumna* (or *avadhūti*) – the central pathway. The first name means very gracious and kind, while the second, *avadhūti,* refers to a lowered head, the unsullied renouncer, the one who has shaken loose. The first variant gives the power received while the second, how to get there. The lowered head gives a hint about *jālandhara bandha* and *prāṇāyāma.*

2. *Sammukha* – the 'even face' covers the entire face, and its activation indicates the state of *pratyāhāra*.

3. *Alāmbuṣa* - 'the line never to be broken' terminates at the tip of the tongue and connects the entire mouth cavity.

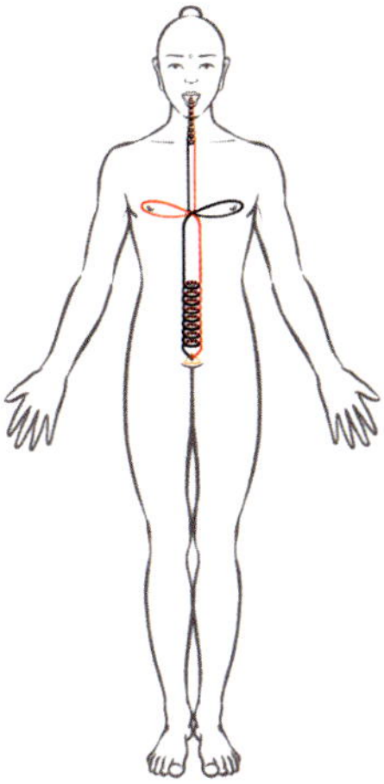

4. *Śaṅkhiṇī* – the conch, in the region of the left breast.

5. *Kūrdari* – the cavern of sound, in the region of the right breast (during their rise, these two *nadīs* spiral around the breasts and terminate in the mouth).

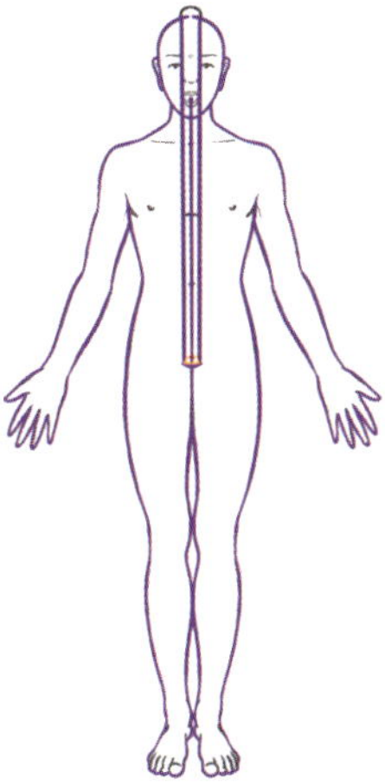

6. *Saraswatī* – the main channel of the *śakti* of sound, ends in the tip of the tongue and spreads throughout the entire body.

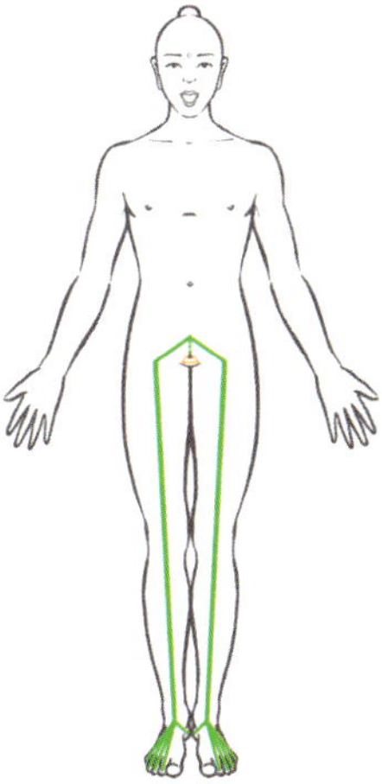

7. *Kuhu* – the new moon extends all the way down to the toes, and ensures the stability and balance of the body and mind.

These seven nadīs are strengthened and controlled with the natural *mūlabandha* that arises in *bhagāsana*.

B. Four *nadīs* stem from the *kandasthana:*

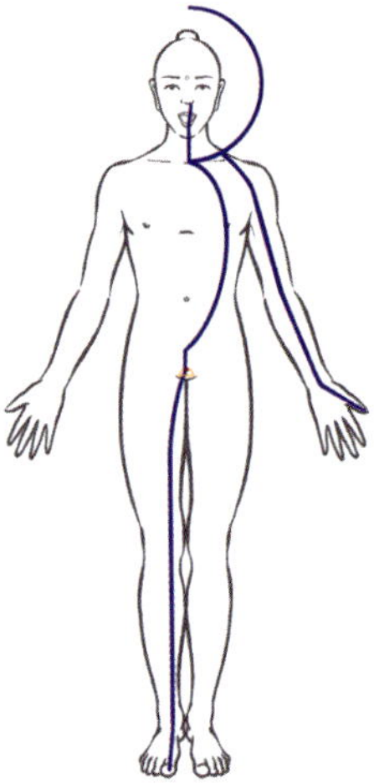

8. *Ida* - the carrier of the moon's light, also called *lalana*, channel, or the swayer of the tongue.

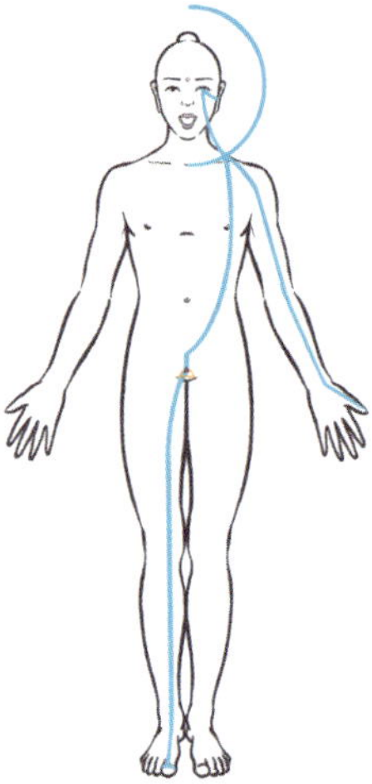

9. *Hastajīvaka* - the hand of long life, or the elongator of the tongue, runs next to and parallel with the *ida nadī.*

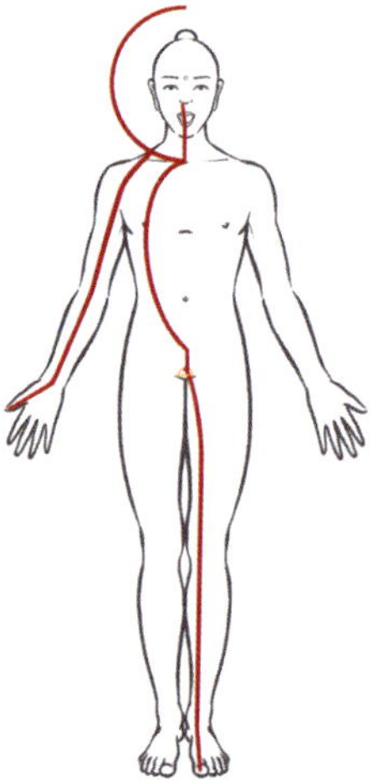

10. *Piṅgala* - the tawny one, carrier of essence, the channel of the sun.

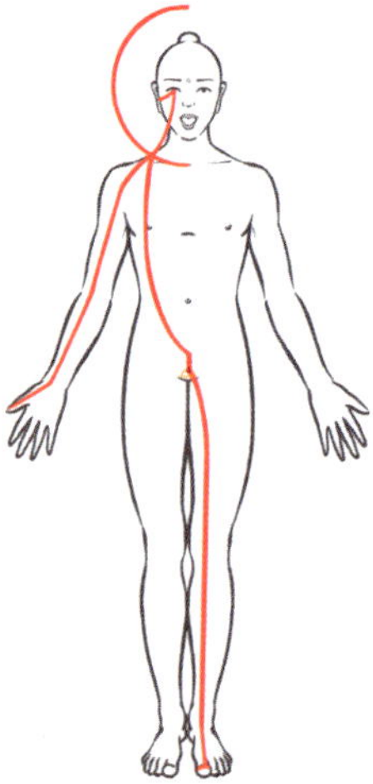

11. *Gāndhārī* - runs next to and parallel with *piṅgala*, and is the carrier of essence received from the mother's milk. This essence is in sound form.

C. The three *nadīs* from the navel region are:

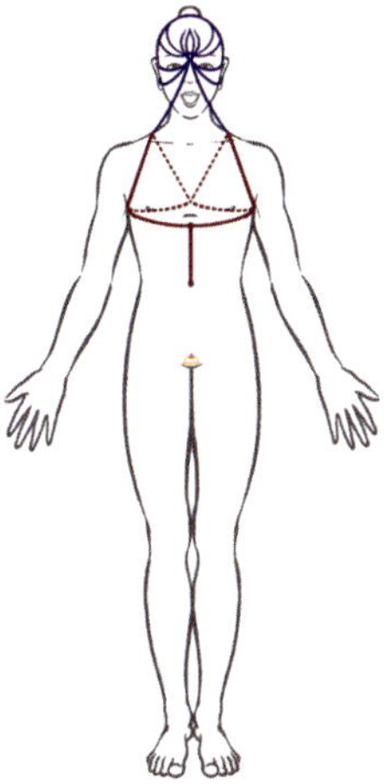

12. *Jaya* – victory over form connecting to the eyes.

13. *Vijaya* – victory over space connecting to the ears.

14. *Vyoma* – the sky or the Milky Way, connecting to the cheeks. It feeds the *vyoma cakra*, which is situated slightly above the third eye, *ajña cakra*, also called *pūrṇagiri*.

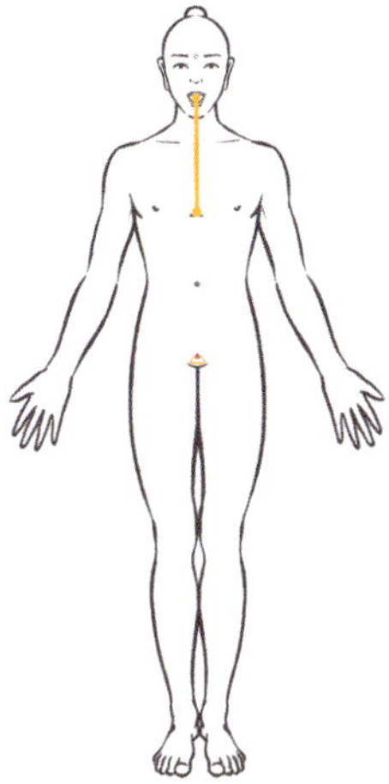

In addition,
15. *Kalpana* – runs from the root of the tongue to the heart and causes the joy of experience.

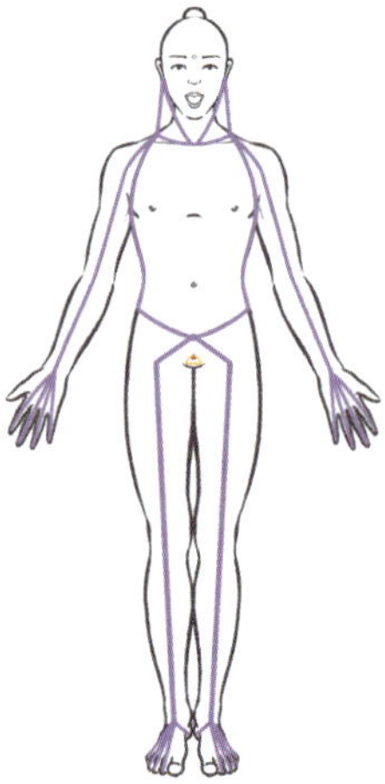

16. *Yaśasvinī* – the eternal flow from the tips of the fingers to the tips of the toes. The meaning behind the name of this *nadī* hints at a connection with the *akanda nadī* (the unrooted *nadī* or *nadī* of the void). The *akanda nadī* is manipulated through *kapāli mudrāsana* (especially the variation of *padmapinda kapāli mudrāsana*) and gives control over the *yaśasvinī nadī*.

This outline of the 16 *nadīs* and their energetic systems provide the foundation for understanding which *āsana-mudras* should be used to harness their energies so that, over time, their essence can be gathered into the single rod of fire within, the *avadhūti nadī*.

With mastery of the *āsanas*, *mudras*, *kriyās* and *prāṇāyāmas* described up to this point, one is in possession of a full range of tools to access this network. For example, *bhagāsana* gives control over the seven *nadīs* that stem from the *mūlādhāra cakra* through *mūlabandha*. *Gorakṣāsana* gives a natural control over the *nadīs* from the *nabhi cakra*, and control over the *viśuddhi cakra* through *jālandhara bandha*. *Kandāsana* centralises the energies of all 16 main *nadīs*.

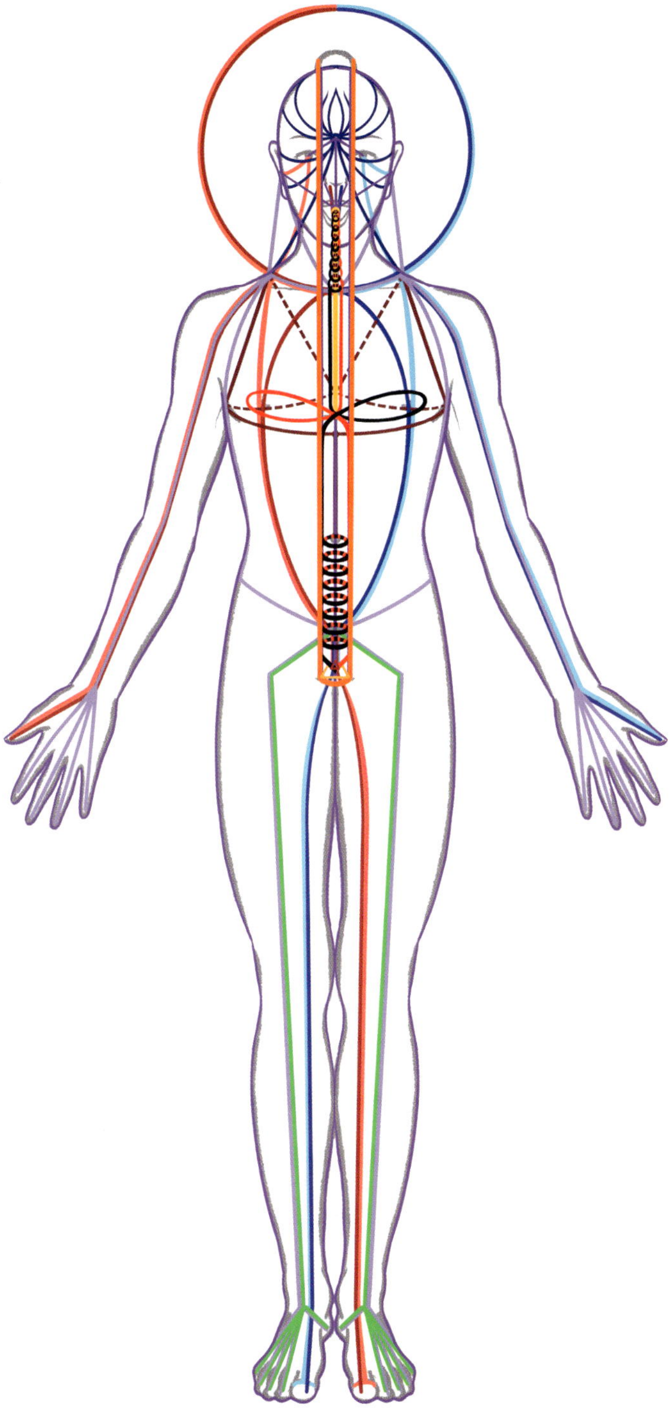

Vajrolī Mudra

Vajrolī mudra is a practical technical activity that belongs to *Rāja Yoga* (the royal path) and acts on the central channel, the pathway of Śakti. There is much puritanical controversy around this *mudra* due to the notoriety of one of the techniques associated with it in which a tube is inserted into the urethra to broaden the passage of the channel. This technique was only used in cases of special difficulty where individuals were unable to master the *āsanas* that achieve the same end. The *āsanas* used for this are *vajrolī mudrāsana* and the three variations of *pāśinī mudra*, which are intense in nature.

All these *āsana-mudras* act upon the urethral passage, and achieve this broadening from within and in a natural manner. The tube technique is an imposed action, an intrusion from the outside with the added drawback of the possibility of infections in both the urethra and the bladder. One should therefore choose one or two of the listed *āsana-mudras* and master them.

Through this mastery one will also gain voluntary control over the energies of the urethra and the bladder, which includes the three lower *cakras* situated between the navel and the perineal floor. The cultivation of this control should be learned under the guidance of an experienced guru. The goal of the practice of *vajrolī mudra* is to increase the power of and control over the *vajra nadī*, since without that power and control the other *mudras* will not yield their full potential.

The term *vajrolī* used for this much-denigrated *mudra* refers to the lightning flash of the thunderbolt (*vajra* is the thunderbolt and *oli* here refers to light). The implication hidden here is that this thunder and lightning presage the fall of rain. In this context it refers to the triggering of the life-sustaining secretions within the body that promote the longevity of the body so that the *sādhaka* yogin can complete his or her destined journey without decline. In this regard three terms are used; *vajrolī*, *sahajolī* and *amarolī*.

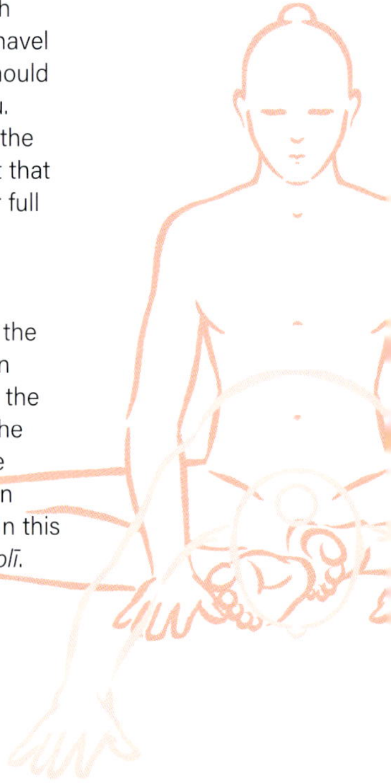

These three comprise a composite action, and to get a better understanding of what lies behind them we can refer to Chapter Seven of Bhavadeva Mishra's text, *Yukta Bhavadeva,* where he states:

There is no difference between them; they differ in names, but their function is identical. When the energies of the sun and moon dissolve into the channel of void at the Kandasthana (slightly above the perineum) it is called Amarolī (the elixir of the immortal light). When Bindu, drop or point is held inside with the help of Yonimudra, it is termed Sahajolī (all powerful light). That natural inner light which causes the bindu to be drawn and raised up is Vajrolī.

Therefore *amarolī* is the result of *prāṇāyāma,* when the life force is centralised by dissolving the opposing energies of night and day. *Sahajolī* refers to the state of *sahajāvastha*, the natural illumined equanimity that results from steadiness in *pratyāhāra* and *dhāranā*. The action of *vajrolī* is the result of the combined power of the bladder and the urethra and is centred near the outer end of the urethra, where the frenulum holds the prepuce in place in men and where the urethra reaches the outer opening of the vagina in women. In the case of men it is called *śiśnabandha* – the binding of the 'tail' (male organ).

Bhavadeva's description of *vajrolī* is intended for practitioner yogins who understand that drawing or sucking one's *bindu* refers to the withdrawal of the energy of the senses and organs of action. It refers specifically to a downward action from the brain into the *mūlādhāra cakra*, which initiates the raising up of the energy from there. This raising is accomplished by the power of the urethra most strongly during the sexual act at the moment of ejaculation, when the energy is contracted from the root of the bladder by the urethra at the base of the head of the penis, causing a deep contraction of the inner space of the anus tightly down against the perineal floor. This is the natural *mūlabandha,* and due to the consequent pressure, the door to the central pathway of *suṣumna* or *avadhūti* opens and at the same time the impulse to release the seed in ejaculation is triggered. It is the power of this impulse that has to be captured, internalised and reabsorbed.

When this is achieved, the *śakti* is awakened, enters the *suṣumna* and rises. All this is cultivated through the practice of *vajrolī mudra*, which helps build the power of the *vajra nadī* (the reproductive energy within the urethra), while the power to reverse the pulsing power of ejaculation is built through the pumping action of *madhyama nauli*.

By these means the yogin utilises the reproductive energy for his or her rise to the self instead of wasting it in sensory gratification. This process is beautifully explained in a passage from the *Rulaka Tantra* to which Gorakṣa refers:

By the contraction of the Adaśakti, the Madhyaśakti awakens and enters the door of Madhya-marga causing the descent of ūrdhvaśakti, to lead to the supreme goal.

Siddha Siddhanta Paddhatih 4.16

It is clear that we are dealing here with one force, which is known by three different names according to its manifestation in different locations and with different functions. *Adaśakti* is the creative outward flowing force that causes the fluctuations of the thinking principle. The contraction of the energy in the *mūlabandha* (*madhyaśakti*), causes first the descent of *ūrdhvaśakti* (*prāṇa*) and then the central rise of the *śakti*. In conclusion, without the cultivation of *vajra nadī* and its *mudra*, the practices of *śakti-calana*, *khecarī* and *śāmbhavī mudras* will be fruitless.

The sexual obsessions of the puritanical critics arise from an insensitivity to the actions of the energetic network and consequent ignorance of its integrity. The origin of the impulse that is at the centre of *vajrolī* lies within the optic thalamus chamber. It is carried through the optic nerve centre at the back section of the brain and is drawn down by the *vajra nadī*. This causes the *mūlabandha*, which contracts and pulls on the olfactory junction where the frenulum of the upper lip and the lower septum meet in line with the root of the upper incisors. As the *vajra nadī* withdraws and gathers the energies of the organs of sense and actions into a single point or *bindu* at the junction point of ejaculation, it is the *khecarī mudra* that causes the reabsorption of the impulse, since the *vajra nadī* and the *saraswatī nadī* (the channel of the tongue) are connected.

The act of procreation carries the hidden essence of form and the rebounding energy of this explosive impulse gives form and power to the *kuṇḍalinī śakti*. This rising form enables her return to the source, at the same time accomplishing the purification of all structures and energies during that rise so that the indweller is liberated from the limits of both the mind and the senses.

Śakti Calanī Mudra

The term *calana* comes from the verb *cal,* to move or agitate, but has also the meaning of turning away, deviating or moving from one's usual course. This latter meaning is most apt here, where the goal is to pull the mind away from its patterns of habitual attachments. By doing so, the senses will follow. To outwit the cleverness of the intellect, the Nāth tantric gurus devised this method of combining the systems of *nauli kriyā* (the churning of the abdominal recti) and *khecarī-mathana* (the churning of the roamer of heaven through the rotation of the tongue). The objective of the churning is to create the sensation of a spiralling rise within, which imitates the rise of *śakti.* This causes the mind to gravitate towards the power of *śakti* and eventually the mind dissolves into it, after some years of effortful strategy.

This part of the journey is not possible unless the physical preparation of *khecarī mudra* has been completed, together with *vajrolī mudra*.

The full *śakti calanī mudra* is carried out in two parts, as detailed below, while seated in *baddha* or *mukta padmāsana*.

Part One - Paridhāna

1. *Bhastrika prāṇāyāma.*

2. *Surya bhedana prāṇāyāma* - (right nostril inhale).

3. *Nauli kriyā* (with *antara kumbhaka*) - the churning of the abdominal recti (from left to right then right to left) with application of the three *bandhas* (*mūla*, *uddiyana* and *jālandhara*), and followed by central pumping of *madhya nauli*. This is concluded by exhaling gently and smoothly through the left nostril. This completes one round of the first part of *śakti calanī mudra.*

Be mindful that the method of *nauli kriyā* undertaken here with *inhalation retention* is exceptionally demanding, and differs in both method and goal from the simpler version with external retention performed at the beginning of the yogic practices. The beginner's version is carried out for purification. The inhalation retention method is used to develop the capacity of absorption in this area. When this has been achieved then the method changes again, but this must be learnt directly from one who has mastered all stages. The method and goal of this process is summed up in the term used to describe it - *paridhāna*. This means the circular wrapping or enfolding of cloth or clothing, and refers here to the inner cloak of completion, which is continuously wrapped and rewrapped around the location of the *kandasthana* through this churning.

All this should all be accompanied by mental repetition of the *khecarī mantra*. An established *sādhaka* should do 10 rounds at sunrise and the same at sunset before beginning the second part of this practice.

Part Two – Mathana

1. *Bhastrika prāṇāyāma* (three to four minutes).

2. *Khecarī mathana* (churning of the tongue) then begins. Inhale through *kākī mudra* and begin to churn the tongue with its tip touching and circling the septum at the root of the nose. This should be done for 25 minutes.

The whole sequence may take 90 minutes to begin with, but as skills improve this will be reduced and as efficacy is achieved the number of churns can also be reduced. After finishing the complete sequence one should remain seated in a state of concentrated withdrawal, allowing the *Prāṇa* to move of its own accord through the circuit that has been set up. When an unbroken flow is achieved the mind will accept and dissolve into it along with all the senses. This marks the awakening of the real *kuṇḍalinī śakti* and the beginning of her slow, rhythmic ascent. At this instant, the whole body will become cold since she sucks all the energy out from it to continue building her own form for the journey to the head.

Before describing the *mathana* in detail, it is good to get a clear picture of the anatomy of the tongue as it is perceived within the science of *khecarī vidyā*. The four important points involved in the churning *mathana* must be properly understood and are as follows.

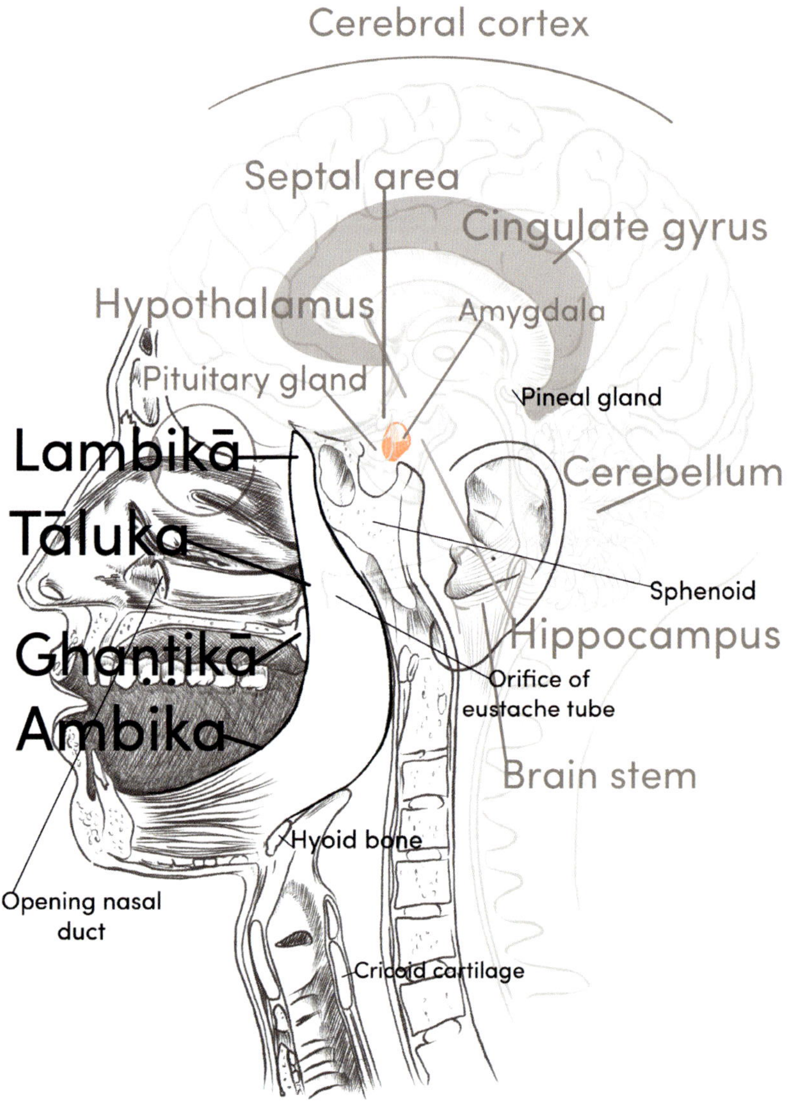

1. *Ambika* (*śakti* – the mother) refers to both the root of the tongue and the frenum, which has been the focus of the milking, lengthening and cutting procedures.

2. *Tāluka* refers to the 10th door, or 10th *adhāra* of the moon, the area of the upper palate where the tip of the tongue is placed, enabling the manipulation of respiration. This is the point on which the tongue is churned and where the tip of the tongue must remain steady after the churning has finished.

3. *Lambikā* is the tip of the tongue.

4. *Ghaṇṭikā* is the uvula. Once the positioning of *lambikā* has been achieved the uvula is subject to a sustained pressure from the back of the tongue. This pressure stimulates an increase in the secretions of the glands situated nearby within the brain. At other times these secretions drip from the uvula onto the surface of the tongue and are swallowed causing thirst and hunger. However when *khecarī mudra* is in place, the secreted fluids flow to the bottom of the mouth to the root of the tongue, where there are three subtle channels that suck up the essence from the fluids. Thus the digestive process is bypassed and the secretions absorbed in this way are referred to collectively as the *amṛta*, or elixir of immortality. The title indicates that they act to prolong the health, strength, and length of the body's life force whilst keeping the body soft and at ease, free from hunger and thirst. Because of this, the practitioner can remain in a deep state of meditation for long periods without needing to move.

Ghaṇṭikā also means bell and this indicates the important role played by the uvula in connection with what is referred to as the *anāhata* or unstruck sound of the heart. The pressure of the back of the middle section of the tongue upon the uvula is responsible for the rise of this sound. The term *trighanti* (triple sounding bell) is also used to refer to the junction point of the uvula and tongue, which is the trigger point for the awakening of *śakti* with *khecarī mudra* and also a cryptic reference to the universal resonating sound principle of A-U-M. This is activated when the tip of the tongue, which is very sharp, hot and penetrating (as it combines the qualities of water and heat) pierces the centre of the 10th door.

The 10th door is the junction point of the three passages coming from the nose, eyes and ears. It is at this point, the *trighanti*, that the contact of the tip of the tongue ignites the central pathway, causing the *suṣumna* or *avadhūti nadī* to light up, and all the other channels to drop away. It is here that the channels of moon and sun unite and dissolve into the central path causing the rise of the universal sound AUM and the opening of the third eye *cakra*, *ajña*. The *sādhaka* who is insufficiently prepared will be shocked to the core by the electrifying explosion as the tip of the tongue thrusts into the centre of the 10th door to the world beyond time and death. This is why one must be patient in laying the groundwork so that when this experience takes place, it can be appropriately processed and absorbed so that it stays with one through the remaining part of the journey.

At this moment of connection a tremendous contraction takes place at the outer end of the urethra. This causes a jolting contraction of the anus (*mūlabandha*), and at the throat (*jālandhara bandha*), which causes a downward pull on the olfactory functions of the nose, the light within the eyes and the space in the ears. This combined action in yogic language is described as the power of *apāna vāyu* pulling *prāṇa*, *udāna*, *samāna* and *vyāna vāyus* down to its domain in the *mūlādhāra cakra*. It is the action in this moment that is referred to as *uṇmani śakti*, the power of trans-mental energy since all outward-flowing processes have been drawn inwards.

The first contact of the tip of the tongue with the upper palatal point, called the 10th door, creates a powerful and lasting impression. It also gives the *sādhaka* the first clear insight into the nature of *bindu* with the experience of instantaneous gathering of the scattered energies of body and mind into a single point. Full realisation of *bindu* will then take up to 12 years of unbroken practice of this churning with the tongue. The action of the churning slowly moves up through the energetic axis like a tornado, gathering and pulling up all the energies as it goes. This gathering aspect is termed *melana*.

Two important rules must be adhered to throughout this process. The first requirement is that the churning is performed from right to left for males and left to right for females. The second is that the tip of the tongue must never stiffen because this will block the action of the *vajra nadī* at the outermost point of the urethra. The entire act of the churning of the tongue on the 10th door is conducted by and manipulated from the *vajra nadī* (junction of return). This coordination is an extremely difficult procedure and tests the individual on all levels.

Modern day representations of the *cakra* system are at once overly complicated and overly simplified since they feed the part of the mind that is most obstructive to entering the state required for this process.

The path of ascent for the *śakti* during the churning, the *suṣumna* or *avadhūti,* extends from the *mūlādhāra*, all the way to the 10th door. In relation to the churning process it is also termed *meru daṇḍa*, which refers to the staff or axis of the mountain that stands at the centre of the cosmos. A warning is concealed here that the very foundation of one's universe will be shaken at the beginning of this process and that one must be ready to face whatever surfaces as one's earth 'quakes'. The next level is termed *meḍhra* and refers to the excretory and generative systems and their organs. This concerns the second *cakra*, the seat of life and water, and all the potentialities and obstacles associated with it. As one works one's way through this murky swamp one realises the extent of the unconscious enslavement of the *śakti*.

The third area is the area of the *nabhi* which is also referred to as *kuṇḍalinī*. Gorakhnāth describes *kuṇḍalinī* as having eight coils. Seven of these are the seven *kośās* or layers of entrapment (described in my first book - *Shadow Yoga*) that are contracted down by the power of the *nabhi* during this process and, in this way, the *nabhi* corrects all mental distortions. The eighth coil is *śakti* in her liberated state. The heart centre is named *kāmarupa* – the seat of the form of desire. This is where the *sādhaka* is confronted with his or her selfish motives. Through the rising of the *śakti* this desire calls forth the divine will which dissolves the individual will.

From the heart centre upwards all the way to the top of the head, is termed *khecarī* which is why it is said that *samādhi* is to be obtained by cultivating the tongue.

During the churning the yogin must listen to a range of sounds as the *śakti* rises through the different layers and stations. It is in the *suṣumna* that the subtlest sound is heard. This sound burns away all sources of disturbances causing a deep state of bliss. When the sound of the moon and the sound of the sun stay within the body, heart, soul and mind, then the universal sound, the source point, and the yogin are one (*Nad-Bind-Yogin*). One has freed *śakti* from her slavery to the senses and the organs of action. We can conclude from this that *uṇmani śakti* is *śabda garbha calana* – the ensnaring of the spoken word through internalisation and reversal back to the source. *Bindu* is the first act of *khecarī mudra*, and the end of all the other *mudras*, since she uses them indirectly according to her requirements. There are no special techniques for *khecarī mudra*. Its secret lies in the doing and the patience to wait for the deity of Khecarī to initiate the waking and the rise. This patience will be the most valuable asset in navigating the seven stations of the *śāmbhavī mudra*.

Chapter 4
Taraṇyali Dīpa Dhyānam: The Floating Lamp Meditation of the Thunder Dragon

The boat that takes both guru and sādhaka across the ocean of worldly life with the brilliance of kuṇḍalinī śakti is called tāraka yoga.

Amanaska Yoga 1:14

O Sage, of the two yogas, tāraka and amanaska, tāraka yoga is the outer yoga, bahiryogamaya, the external divine illusory power.

Amanaska is antarmudra the internal gesture, the real yoga.

Amanaska Yoga 2:2

Tāraka yoga is that which is accomplished with the mind and the body while *Amanaska Yoga* is without or beyond the mind and is therefore the famed *śāmbhavī mudra* (Śiva's benevolent gesture) with the aim inwards and the gaze outwards. The appearance of this *mudra* signifies the arrival of Kuṇḍalinī Śakti emanating forth from Śambhu. Though deeply hidden in most, she is the natural birthright of every human being. The self knowledge that reveals her, called *amanaska*, is acquired through the various yogic sciences, with the grace and understanding of the gurus and is for the benefit of all. The nature of *tāraka* is *samanaska* (with mind) and *sakala* (with all its constituent parts). These constituents, like the 10 pranic winds, the organs of sense and actions and all the body parts are mortal and should be renounced. *Amanaska* is *nirmanaska*, beyond or without mind, and *niṣkala*, single without parts; it is effortless and should be practiced.

The first two stages of the *Taraṇyali Tridhā Dhyānam*, together with their *samādhi*, are *samanaska* and *sakala*, as they utilise the constructs of the mind and the body with all their parts and energetic networks. As we have seen, the culmination of that process is the mastery of the *khecarī mudra* which is also referred to in the *Amanaska Yoga*.

When the yogi remains absorbed for 13 days continuously, he or she gains the power known as Khecarī Siddhi (the soarer of the pathways of heaven) just by thinking of it.

Amanaska Yoga 1.78

This implies that one who has managed the mastery of *khecarī mudra* can now let go of all that has been practised and accumulated in the first two stages and is ready to enter the training of the crowning procedures of the *śāmbhavī mudra*. The importance of making these changes is reiterated at the end of the second chapter.

The chanting of OṂ and other mantras, the methods of controlling prāṇa (āsana, mudra, prāṇāyāma etc) and concentration on internal states must be given up since they are all mental delusions pertaining to the body. They should all have been previously mastered and understood. From this point only amanaska bhava (transcendent being) should be practised, which is beyond the limits of body, speech and mind.'

Amanaska Yoga 2:114.

To withdraw from all the practices that have been utilised in the *Taraṇyali Krantam* and *Taraṇyali Kriyā* without repercussions, a bridging activity is essential. It is easy to panic at this point, to lose one's bearings and flail around looking for anything to fill the gap that has opened up.

The ignorant person not knowing the ātma tattva (self) wanders among the scriptures searching for it, though it is there within him or her just as a foolish shepherd searches for a lamb in the well while the lamb is held under his armpit.

Amanaska Yoga 2:20

This bridging activity is slow and, compared to the numerous and elaborate practices left behind, deceptively simple. If the necessary preliminaries have been completed then four rounds of *nadī śuddhi prāṇāyāma* are sufficient to withdraw and retain all energies from the organs of sense, and the extremities of the body, and gather them into a single point - *bindu*.

One whose sight, breath, prāṇa and mind remains still and stable without the support of their objects is really a yogi, a guru, worthy of service.

Amanaska Yoga 2:46

As described in the introduction, these necessary preliminaries include the full apprehension of the 24 *nadīs* or power accumulation sites. The initiate *sādhaka* will have mentally travelled through the network of these sites at the beginning of the *prāṇam* performed before every practice. Through repeated daily application of *yoginī-nyāsa-vidhim* (the placement of power through touch) there should now be a full engagement with and responsiveness to these sites and to the flow between them and the three main channels.

The network of these flows is as follows.

Group One

The *nadīs* (streams) of the enlightened mind.

Mind: the indivisible *nadī*, the passage of the subtle form at the hairline (1) at the tip of the head (fontanelle) (2), feeds the right ear (3) the seat of compassion and kindness which points to the left temple (4) the inheritance of the spirits of the fathers and the ancestors (manes) that sinks into the left ear (5), the hidden channel which feeds *śakti* resting upon the third eye (6), the channel of truth that controls the gates of the two eyes (7), whose weight is borne and carried upon the shoulders (8). Hence eight pathways of the mind.

Group Two

The *nadīs* of enlightened speech (the streams that feed the tongue).

At the armpits (1) sits the power of obstruction pointing to the entrance at the breasts (2) that leads to motion at the heart (3), which pours down into the navel (4) and feeds *kuṇḍalinī* that becomes the power of the night with its seat at the tip of the nose (5), the supplier of coolness to the mouth (6), causing heat at the throat (7), which spreads the power of joy at the cheeks (8).

The 16 *nadīs* of these two groups pour their contents into, and are housed within the eight *nadīs* of the third group, that of enlightened form.

Group Three

The power of excellence lies at the tip of the sexual organ (1), which is weighed down at the anus (2), that disrupts the energetic flow at the root of the thighs (3), causing the split of unity at the calves (4), yet also the rise of absolute beauty through the eight fingers and eight toes (the 16 digits of the moon) (5). These 16 open the source of *rasa* at the junction of the shins and ankles (6), while its cooking is achieved through the two thumbs and two big toes (7), which render the smoothness of the knees (8) that are the source of power of the pure mind.

After the *yoginī-nyāsa-vidhim* and the *prāṇam* one sits in *baddha padmāsana* and performs *bhastrika*, followed by four rounds of *nadī śuddhi prāṇāyāma* (alternate nostril breathing) with breath retentions after inhalation. The retention is accompanied at first by a single repetition of the *khecarī mantra* – after some time this can be extended to two and eventually three repetitions. One should be seated in *baddha padmāsana*, as *nadī śodhana*, purification of the *nadīs* (*ida*, *piṅgala* and *suṣumna*) involves the internal circuits of *prāṇa vayu* and very little external air will be drawn in. As the physical part of *khecarī* has been acquired by this stage, the tip of the tongue should be used to open and close the *nadīs*. One must release the breath through the *ida nadī* and then draw in through the same *nadī*, followed by *kumbhaka* and then out and in through the *piṅgala nadī*, retaining the breath before releasing through the *ida nadī*. This is one round. The three *bandhas* are utilised at their appropriate places. Four full rounds of this should be performed.

After this yoga *mudrāsana* should be performed and one should stay with the head and torso down in this position until any tension is released. This is followed by *tolāsana* to remove any sluggishness that may have accumulated, after which the practices of *śāmbhavī mudra* are begun. The only other *āsana* that is of use here is *vajrāsana* (*siddhāsana*). The *khecarī mudra* is sustained but without the auxiliary practices like churning used before, and with the tip of the tongue in contact with the ridge of the 10th door, which is also referred to as the Bolt of Brahma.

When, following the dissolution of the three *granthis* (knots), the powers of these 24 *nadīs* are united with the eight powers of the heart through the practice of *khecarī* and *śakticalanī mudras*, then access to the secret web will be granted to the 'net holder', the yogin.

Reflecting on this, one can begin to grasp the hidden power of *baddha padmāsana*. By grasping the big toes from behind, all the 32 powers are pulled into a central position so that the naturally occurring obstruction areas are dissolved. This renders the subtle force free and detached from the physical structures and allows the melding of the subtle force into a single pillar of light. This is however no easy task and requires persistence and tremendous endurance in the face of many discomforts, even for those who may possess natural ability in the outer form of this *āsana*.

Śāmbhavī Mudra

Before we enter into a detailed description of this mudra it is good to take a closer look at the term *tāraka* that is used to describe all those practices that carry one to the brink of the *śāmbhavī mudra*. Among the many subsidiary meanings of this word are star, beam of light, lamp, eye and ferryman or one who carries the departed from the banks of this life to the shoreless beyond.

By working with the physical structure through the gross *kriyās*, *āsanas* and *mudras* of the *Taraṇyali Krantam* and

Taraṇyali Kriyā, the fire principle is automatically increased since all forms belong to fire and are perceived through the eyes. When these forms are clarified and their energy withdrawn, it manifests as inner light which rises into the higher regions of the mental planes, where the physical counterparts cannot go. In these higher realms it continues to evolve and transform through different layers until it dissolves into the limitless infinite. This is what is hinted at behind the term *tāraka*.

The other term used in the *Amanaska Yoga* text for this preparatory yoga is *pūrva tāraka yoga*. The basic meaning of *pūrva* is previous, but it refers also to the east, the source of light and so the beginning of time. *Pūrva* is also used to denote a period of 8,400,000 years (this number being used to represent the immeasurable or unlimited, as in the 8,400,000 *āsanas* of Śiva) and so encompasses the entirety of experience and existences since the beginning of time. The implication is that the individual contains the whole universe within himself or herself, and this provides the mind with infinite opportunities to get lost or confused in its wanderings

As the *sādhaka* approaches the far shore of this *tāraka yoga* they carry the lamp of inner light that has been extracted from this vast number of experiences and practices, which must all now be left behind.

The idea of the departure beyond all shores is enough to fill an elephant with fear, let alone a small-framed human being. However, by mastering the *Taraṇyali Krantam* and *Taraṇyali Kriyā* one is able to render the mind still, and armed with the pillar of inner light one is able to let go of attachments and go beyond the limited fabrications of the mind. One may live a fearless existence in the wisdom of this light until the time of the natural departure from this earthly form.

The seven stages of the *śāmbhavī mudra* are diagnostic in nature and reveal where one stands in relation to the ultimate truth in the present moment. The aims and gazes are a natural outcome of the cultivation of the various practical fields of activity. Unfortunately, *śāmbhavī mudra* is now portrayed as an imposed technique due to poor translations of the texts by those who lack practical knowledge of the field. The instruction is given that one should turn the physical gaze of the eyes to the third eye centre and aim at the central path. This is an action imposed by the mind – *samanaska* (with the mind) and not *amanaska* (beyond mind). The *śāmbhavī mudra* is a natural process of awareness in which the mind continually sweeps over the mental fields and the remaining residual attachments of the mind, ever alert to the changes that are triggered in them. One must remember that although *khecarī mudra* is now mastered and *śakti* is on the rise, she will not expose herself fully to a corrupted mind as this will cause her to fall back into the slavery of the senses.

The Seven Stages

1. *Bahirlakṣya-Bahirdṛṣṭi*

External Aim and External gaze

This takes place as soon as the yogin decides to do *padmāsana*: both the attention of the aim and the gaze flow outwards. If there are no obstructions within the posture, both the aim and the gaze will loosen and move towards the second level. However, if mastery of and ease in the *āsana* are lacking, aim and gaze will remain on the outside until corrected. If the mind decides to ignore this and force onwards, this reveals the underlying impatience and ruthlessness of the individual. On the other hand, if both the aim and gaze begin to move towards the next level and yet the mind holds back, this shows a mind overshadowed by egotistical attachment to control. Most *sādhakas* will suffer the consequences of one or both of these afflictions.

2. *Antarlakṣya-Antardṛṣṭi*

Internal Aim and Internal Gaze

The first stage is concerned with observation of the anatomical framework and its physical safety: both the aim and gaze are earthbound. The second stage is concerned with observation of the physiological activities within the anatomical framework, and their level of ease or obstruction.

If there is obstruction, both the aim and gaze will be disturbed, but if there is ease, both the gaze and the aim will remain steady and central. When the harmonious feeling spreads throughout the entire structure the mind can either choose to move towards the next stage or to remain in a state of intoxication until the harmony breaks down and the mind is left in doubt and uncertainty.

3. *Bahirlakṣya-Antardṛṣṭi*

External Aim and Internal Gaze

This is the sign of equanimous unobstructed physical harmony and shows that the two earlier stages of the Thunder Dragon were truly mastered. The *sādhaka* yogin is ready to soar the mental planes of the regions of *khecarī*, but the difficulty encountered here is one of attachment and procrastination. There is an attachment to this feeling of well-being accompanied by an anxiety about letting go.

> This is the early appearance of the fear of death latent within the physical gross structure of the body. If this is the case one must not try to push on but instead sustain this stage until one understands the source of one's uncertainty.

This state is best described as marching on the spot.

These first three stages are preliminary stages of evaluation to test whether the field of consciousness has been properly prepared and cultivated so that it can rise above the delusory mundane world and the academic intellect. When these are transcended, the consciousness is led by *buddhi*, the intuitive intellect that exists in the *apara* shoreless condition. This subtle all-pervasive power of cognition is pure understanding and is eternally Śiva's natural state. When the state of *buddhi* is present, the aim and gaze will indicate this and *buddhi* only comes to the foreground when the early signs of the fear of death have been dissolved by the *sādhaka* yogin.

4. *Antarlakṣya-Bahirdṛṣṭi*

Internal Aim and External Gaze

This is the beginning of the true *śāmbhavī mudra* and the first manifestation of what is termed the *dhārāyantra* (water 'machine' or fountain). The device of the *dhārāyantra* (or *radayantra*) is derived from the story in which Arjuna, the master archer, and hero of the Mahābharata, takes part in an archery competition to win Princess Draupadi's hand in marriage.

The contest involves a revolving target in the shape of a fish suspended high above a well. The contending archer has to hit this target with bow and arrow held above the back of his head while kneeling and looking down with his gaze fixed upon the image of the turning fish reflected in the surface of the water at the bottom of the well. Arjuna's inner aim is upwards but his head and outer sight are held down towards the water. So in this fourth stage of the *śāmbhavī mudra* the head is held down in *jālandhara bandha* while the inner sight is aimed at the 12 petalled lotus, which is situated above the third eye, below the 14th *adhāra* of the moon and behind the middle of the forehead. This is the seat of the *para tattva* that is Śiva, and is also referred to as the *pūrṇagiri* or highest peak or temple and the point 'beyond aims'. At the same time the outer gaze is held to a point level with the *svādhiṣṭhāna* one arm length downwards from the eyes, which are kept half open, half closed.

The hidden message of this imagery is that insight to the higher truth is held below, reflected in the centre of the water element, which is the seat of *prāṇa*, the life breath. This is the basis for the statement, often quoted in the yoga texts, that the soul is worshipped at the *mūlādhāra cakra* with *prāṇa* as the arrow and Śiva the target.

The *sādhaka* now stands at the entrance door of Śiva's inner-most temple but must wait for the rise of the *kuṇḍalinī śakti* and the accompanying unfolding of innate wisdom. The success of the rest of the journey is dependent upon maintaining patient attentiveness to allow this process to take its natural course. The *sādhaka* has been in this position before at the very beginning of his or her journey. The stand they took in the void then was in a state of innocence, but is now taken consciously and with foreknowledge. This conscious apprehension grants them entry to the meditation of void - *śūnya dhyāna*, the most important part of *laya yoga sādhana* and *Amanaska Yoga*, also known as *bhavatita dhyāna* - transcendental meditation.

5. *Bahirlakṣya-Pratibimbadṛṣṭi*

External Aim with Gaze fixed on the Shadow of the Aim

The entry to this next stage comes with a shock since the eyeballs suddenly and strongly contract, rolling upwards with the pupils focused towards the centre of the third eye. This contraction is orchestrated through the *vajra nadī* causing a jolted *mūlabandha* that pulls on the inner corners of the eyes, narrows the *nadī* at the root of the nose and sucks the tip of the tongue hard against the triple junction of nose, eyes and ears. Termed the Bolt of Brahma, this causes the eyeballs to remain turned up and steady in their new position with the eyelids neither fully shut nor fully open. The *sādhaka* will realise that the preparation for this action took place during the cultivation of *yoga mudrāsana* in *baddha* and *mukta padmāsanas*. As the necessary energetic circuit has already been set up in this way, when the opportune moment within the rise of consciousness presents itself, then the Bolt of Brahma will be triggered.

While the aim is fixed in this way, the gaze should be directed to the shadow of the aim; shadow refers to the the fear that arises when, through the Bolt of Brahma, one enters Śiva's temple. The fear reveals the presence of attachments and residual karmas. The *sādhaka* must learn to stay with their gaze attentive to this shadow as the *śakti* works her way up from the *mūlādhāra cakra*. Her rise will disclose the residual karmas present at each *cakra* and she will stay at that centre until the *sādhaka* becomes fully conscious of them so that the attachment falls away and she moves to the next level. This continues all the way to the heart (*anāhata cakra*) where the *sādhaka* is still attached to the emotional states of the outer form. Once these are cleared the *sādhaka* yogin is taken to the inner sanctum of the temple, which is the next stage.

6. *Antarlakṣya-Pratibimbadṛṣṭi*

Internal Aim with Gaze fixed on the Shadow of the Aim

The only change here is that the aim and gaze are fused, and internally directed, indicating that one has detached and moved away from the physical form. The shadow remaining here is not fear for the safety of the physical form itself but the unconscious fear of the loss of the mind, the mental sheath of the body. This shift also marks the entry of *śakti* into the base of the throat (*viśuddhi cakra*), the centre of the final purification and the lower border of the *pūrṇagiri*. The remaining task of her journey upwards is to dissolve the final traces of lingering fear held in the three *granthis* or knots so that the soul itself is freed from its burden of attachment. This stage is referred to in the texts as learning to die without the body's death.

7. *Lakṣyatita-Lakṣya*

The Aim Beyond Aim

As one enters this final stage, the tip of the tongue becomes perfectly still at the Bolt of Brahma yet, at the same time, the *sādhaka* is flooded with a feeling that something more must take place before one can be fully released into the vastness of the pathways of heaven. It is now that one is able to fully dissolve the three *granthis*, the deep knots that tie one to the world of appearances. They are *brahma granthi*, the lord of creation that rules over the three lower *cakras*; *viṣṇu granthi*, the lord of sustenance that lives in the heart region; and *rudra granthi*, the terrible knot that binds one to the objective world of name and form. The first knot imprisons one through attachment to sexuality and its manifold layers of desire. The second knot imprisons through attachment to family and friends, and all that goes with them. The third knot ties one to the material world with all its false and deceptive propensities, and is called the terrible knot because its loosening explodes one into the void beyond all

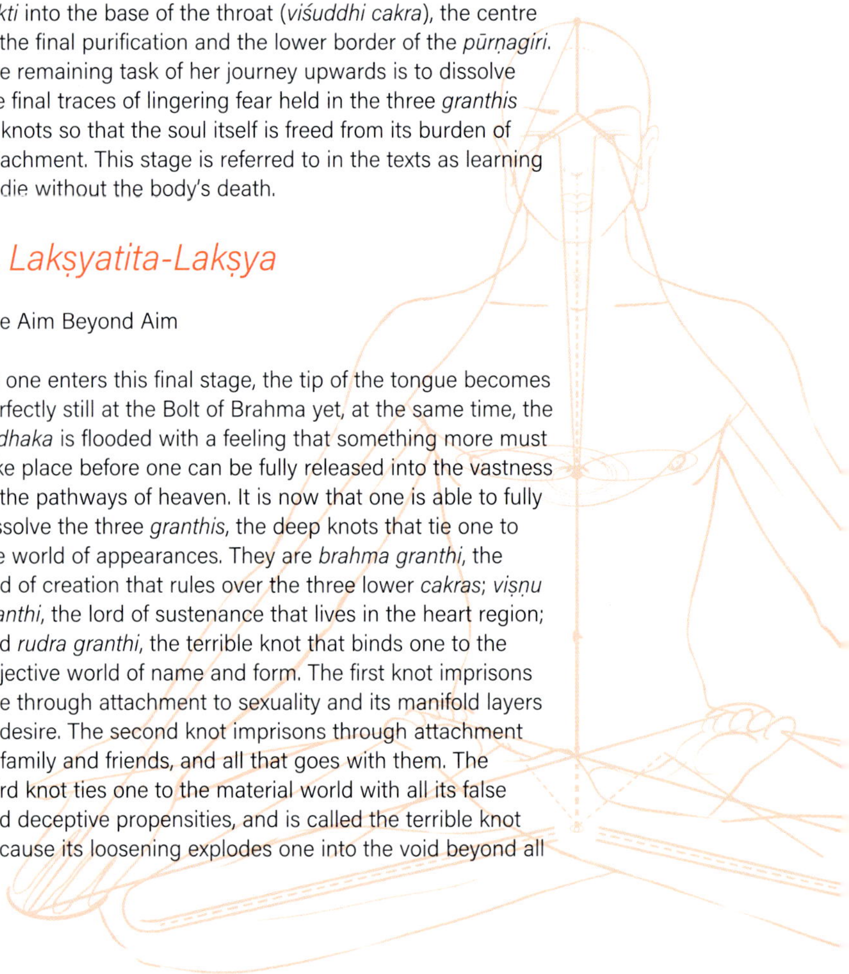

aims, and the grip of the mind and the senses.
All of this takes place at *bindu visarga*, near the tuft of the hair known as the *candra maṇḍala* (circle of the moon). It is at this point of light that one must linger until full consciousness of the content of the three knots brings their loosening. This begins to unfold the moment the tongue is in touch with the ridge of the Bolt of Brahma. At that precise moment the *prāṇa* begins to flow through both the *ida* and *piṅgala* channels, which indicates that the *suṣumna nadī* is at work, carrying the pranic force upwards towards the *candra maṇḍala*. This pranic flow is the true *ujjayi prāṇāyāma* (victorious breath) and not the ubiquitous present day huffing and puffing methods of forceful and imposed breathing. As the *kuṇḍalinī* reaches the *candra maṇḍala*, the tongue slips away from the ridge of the Bolt of Brahma and spontaneously begins to churn freely in the void. In this moment it becomes clear that *khecarī* and *śāmbhavī mudras* are one and the same. *Khecarī* is the means and *śāmbhavī* is the perception of the means.

This marks the completion of Śakti's journey. She has joined her Lord Śiva and all feeling of separation has ended in the realm beyond the mind. The soul is bathed in the eternal light of wisdom and the *sādhaka* is now a complete yogin. The entry into the deep state of merging is spontaneous and can persist for an hour, a day, a month or even longer. It is during this period of absorption that the different gifts or *siddhis* (the so called 'powers') manifest according to individual karma. The *tantras* warn that one must not flaunt these *siddhis*, as the fall from this height will be endless and irreversible.

The return to the mundane world is also not a simple matter. It can be compared to the situation of the soldier, returning from war without deprogramming, who finds himself living in his own hell.

One must ease back into the world of ordinary life by consciously retracing each step taken in the rising, so as to avoid the shock of a crash landing. In time, and with repetition, these transitions become easier. Eventually just the thought of the 'beyond' state will take the yogin there.

The return will also become a simple matter of individual choice taken in rhythm with one's destiny.

When this seventh stage has been attained there is no longer any need for specific procedures since the perfection of the *siddhi* state comes solely through deeper penetration into *śāmbhavī mudra*. If and when the yogin becomes aware of any further residual attachments, *śakti* will spontaneously consume the energy of that attachment at the associated *cakra* and use it to fuel her journey upwards.

One who is established like this in *śāmbhavī* and *khecarī mudras* gains full and spontaneous access to the equilibrium of the *dhārāyantra* state and freedom from the cycle of birth and death (*jīvanmukti*).

With firm fist upward, gaze held downwards, piercing upwards through the cakras with head bent down (in jālandhara) by application of the dhārāyantra one gains the jīvanmukti.

Amanaska Yoga 2.16

As in the fountain where power is constantly generated to force the water upwards to the fountain head while the constant falling shower is gathered to replenish the pump at the base, so here, with aim up, are the *prāṇas* made to enter the *suṣumna nadī* and surge up towards the *sahasrāra cakra* even as the gaze is held down by the power of the *mūlabandha*. The aim here is that of Śakti and the gaze is that of Śiva; they are one and this is a purely spontaneous state in which the individual mind has no part to play.

As long as the truth of being is not realised it is impossible to fully restrain the mind. With tattva darśana the mind comes to rest like a crow alighting on the mast of a ship in the middle of the ocean.

Amanaska Yoga 2.76

Here ends the *Taraṇyali Tridhā Dhyānam* of the Yogin Sundernāth. (Shandor Remete)

Mudra – gesture is the power of *śakti* that will melt whatever has been sealed (*mudrita*). The sealed is that which has been hidden by the double natured power of consciousness, which is both inferior and reductive yet supreme.

Ūrdhva Tāṇḍava

Photos of Emma Balnaves

Talasamsphotitam

Kuñcitam

Jade Lady

Padmāsana

Jade Lady Waving

Kandāsana

Conclusion

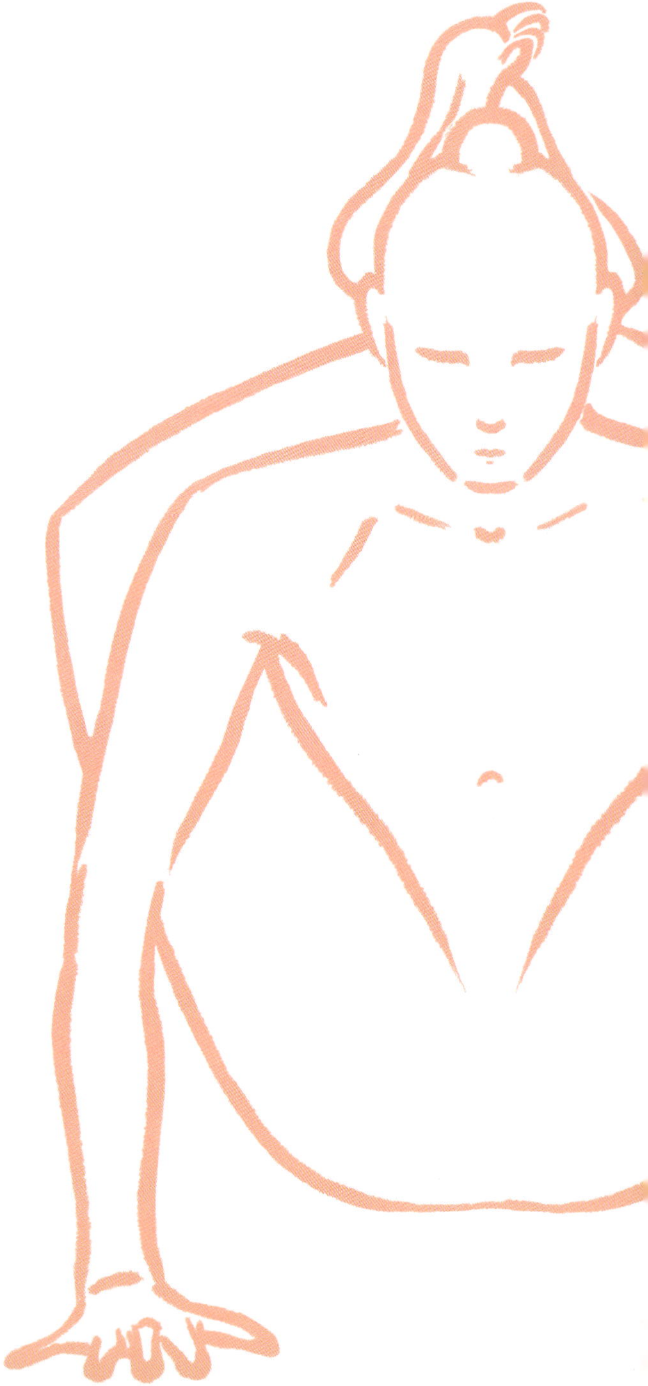

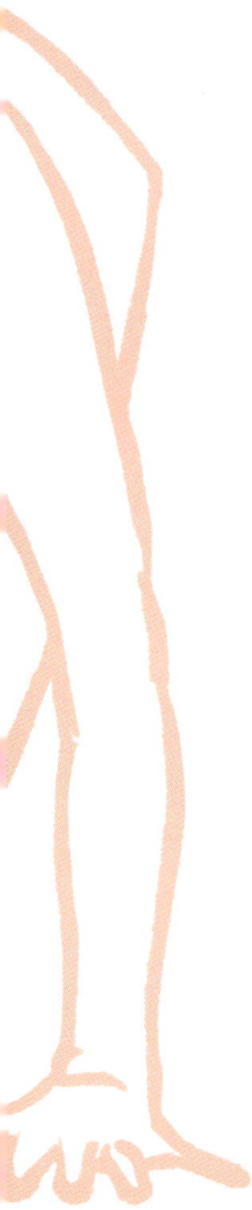

In this era, the seeker of yoga is soon lost among a multitude of schools competing for their attention with every kind of gimmick. If they turn to the many yoga texts now available in translation, their confusion is only deepened by encyclopaedic compilations that are little more than lists, or by manuals written originally as an aid to aural transmission in a cryptic terminology now impenetrable. As we have seen, the journey is a complex process and what at first may seem separate activities are different facets of an integrated process of unfolding. This is sometimes called the *mahā marga* (great path) or *mahā yoga* (great yoga) and is comprised of *mantra*, *laya*, *rāja* and *haṭha yogas*.

Haṭha yoga refers to the full expression and equilibrium of the *ida* and *piṅgala nadīs* through the drawing together of the energetic network of the body by means of *āsana*, *kriyā*, *mudra* and *kumbhaka*. *Mantra yoga* refers to the integration of *manas* (mind) and *prāṇa* through the internal use of sound and mantra. *Laya yoga* is the absorption of mind through the sense of internal touch brought to perfection through *khecarī* and *śāmbhavī mudras*, and *rāja yoga* is the mastery of the life force within the *avadhūti nadī* by means of *vajrolī mudra*.

Each step requires great care and discernment. Knowing what to do and when to do it is the key. For all but one in a million this will require a guru and, without exception, everyone will require the grace of the deity of Khecarī.

Once the journey has been completed all that is necessary to sustain the energy and health of the body and the unity of the organism are a few of the *mudras* interwoven with *prāṇāyāma*. That choice rests with the individual.

Bibliography

Amanaska Yoga - Mahamahopadhyaya, Dr Brahma Mitra Awasthi with English translation by Shri Bajaranga. Singh Swami Keshawananda Yoga Samsthana-Prakashana. Delhi 1987

Matsyendra Samhitha - translation by Poonthottam Chandramohan. Original text, published by the Asiatic Society, Calcutta

Gorakṣaśatakam - translated by Swami Kuvalayananda, Sr.S.A. Shukla. Published: Kaivalyadhama, 2006